Macmillan/McGraw-Hill

Math Connects
2

Reteach and Skills Practice Workbook

 Macmillan/McGraw-Hill

TO THE TEACHER   These worksheets are the same ones found in the Chapter Resource Masters for *Math Connects, Grade 2*. The answers to these worksheets are available at the end of each Chapter Resource Masters booklet.

The McGraw-Hill Companies

 Macmillan/McGraw-Hill

Send all inquiries to:
Macmillan/McGraw-Hill
8787 Orion Place
Columbus, OH 43240

ISBN: 978-0-02-107303-0
MHID: 0-02-107303-1   *Reteach and Skills Practice Workbook, Grade 2*

Printed in the United States of America.

1 2 3 4 5 6 7 8 9 10 079 14 13 12 11 10 09 08

CONTENTS

iv

Name _____

Reteach

Tens and Ones

Another name for ten ones is one ten.

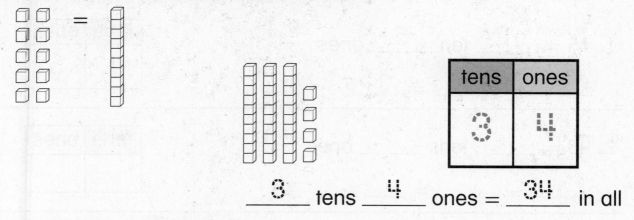

_____3_____ tens _____4_____ ones = _____34_____ in all

Count how many tens and ones. Write the number.

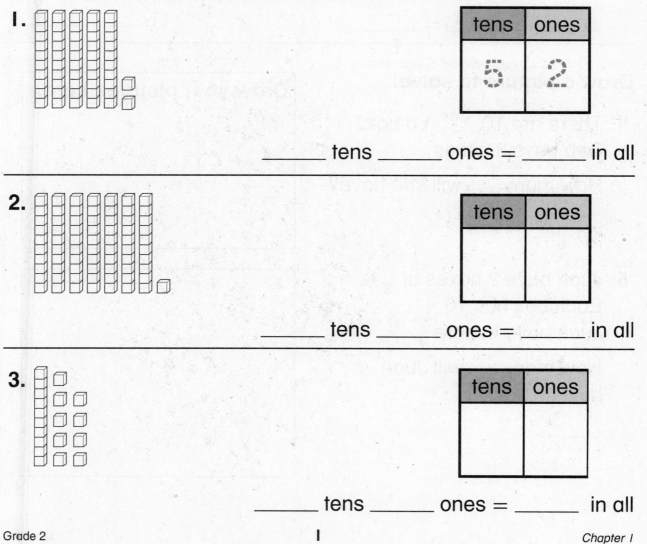

1.

tens	ones
5	2

_____ tens _____ ones = _____ in all

2.

tens	ones

_____ tens _____ ones = _____ in all

3.

tens	ones

_____ tens _____ ones = _____ in all

Name _____

Skills Practice

Tens and Ones

Write how many ones. Then write how many tens.

1. 15 = ___1___ ten ___5___ ones

   ___10___ + ___5___ = ___15___

tens	ones
1	5

2. 43 = _____ tens _____ ones

   _____ + _____ = _____

tens	ones

3. 66 = _____ tens _____ ones

   _____ + _____ = _____

tens	ones

Draw a picture to solve.

4. There are 10 ✏ in a box.
   Deb buys 3 boxes.

   How many ✏ will she have?

   _____ pencils

5. Juan buys 2 boxes of 🍎.
   Each box has 10 🍎.
   Juan buys 4 more 🍎.

   How many 🍎 will Juan
   have in all?

   _____ 🍎

Draw your pictures here.

Name _____

Reteach

Place Value to 100

Each digit in a number has a value.

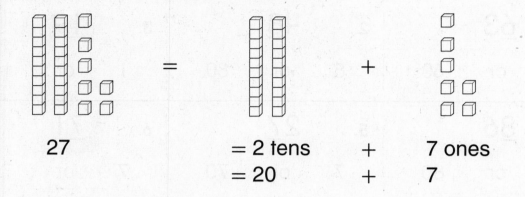

27   = 2 tens   +   7 ones
            = 20   +   7

Circle the value of the underlined digit.

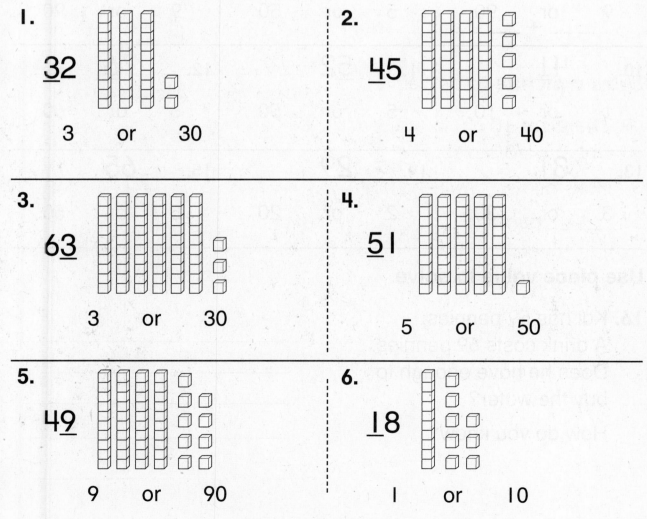

1.   <u>3</u>2

3   or   30

2.   <u>4</u>5

4   or   40

3.   6<u>3</u>

3   or   30

4.   <u>5</u>1

5   or   50

5.   4<u>9</u>

9   or   90

6.   <u>1</u>8

1   or   10

1-2

Skills Practice

Place Value to 100

Circle the value of the underlined digit.

1. 6̲3

    6   or   60

2. 4̲8̲

    8   or   80

3. 1̲9

    1   or   10

4. 8̲6

    8   or   80

5. 2̲7̲

    7   or   70

6. 7̲1

    7   or   70

7. 59̲

    9   or   90

8. 15̲

    5   or   50

9. 9̲3

    9   or   90

10. 41̲

    1   or   10

11. 5̲2

    5   or   50

12. 76̲

    6   or   60

13. 3̲1

    3   or   30

14. 2̲9

    2   or   20

15. 65̲

    5   or   50

Use place value to solve.

16. Kai has 59 pennies.
    A drink costs 69 pennies.
    Does he have enough to
    buy the water?

    How do you know? _____

1-3

Reteach (1)

Problem-Solving Strategy: Use Logical Reasoning

Three boys ride bicycles.
Pat rides behind Bill.
Bill rides behind Rob.
Who rides in front?

Step 1 **Understand** ➤	**What do I know?** Pat rides behind Bill. Bill rides behind Rob. **What do I need to find?** I need to find _____.
Step 2 **Plan** ➤	**How will I find the answer?** I can use logical reasoning.
Step 3 **Solve** ➤	**Use logical reasoning.** The first clue: Pat is behind Bill. Write the order. _____, _____ The second clue: Bill is behind Rob. Write the order. _____, _____ Who rides in front? _____
Step 4 **Check** ➤	Is my answer reasonable? Yes No

Name _____

Reteach (2)

Problem-Solving Strategy: Use Logical Reasoning

Use logical reasoning to solve.	**Show your work here.**
1. Kris, Nick, and Lara share a bus seat. Kris sits by the window. Lara is not sitting next to Kris. Who sits in the middle?	
_____	
2. Tim, Emma, Ling, and Cory run a race. Emma is first. Ling is after Tim. Tim is not second. Who is second?	
_____	
3. Pete, Ed, and Jane buy ice cream. Their cones have 1, 2, and 3 scoops. Pete has 2 scoops. Ed has more scoops than Pete. How many scoops does Jane have?	
_____ scoop	
4. Juan, Mia, and Wes pick 3 cards. Their numbers are 8, 5, and 1. Juan picks number 5. Wes does not pick number 8. Who picks number 8?	
_____	

Name _____

Skills Practice

Problem-Solving Strategy: Use Logical Reasoning

Use *logical reasoning* to solve. | **Show your work here.**

1. Zach, Alex, and Jen are on stage. Zach is on the left. Jen is not next to Zach. Who is in the middle?

   _____

2. Lori, Sara, Jill, and Ann are in line. Lori is first. Sara is after Lori. Ann is before Jill. Who is fourth?

   _____

3. Muhammed, Maria, and Chan have tickets. They are numbered 1, 2, and 3. Maria has number 2. Chan does not have number 3. Who has number 3?

   _____

4. Faye, Dan, and Trey are wearing soccer shirts. The shirts are numbered 2, 6, and 7. Dan has number 6. Trey's number is greater than Dan's. Who has number 2?

   _____

Name _____

Reteach

Read and Write Numbers

You can write word names for numbers.

1	one	11	eleven	30	thirty
2	two	12	twelve	40	forty
3	three	13	thirteen	50	fifty
4	four	14	fourteen	60	sixty
5	five	15	fifteen	70	seventy
6	six	16	sixteen	80	eighty
7	seven	17	seventeen	90	ninety
8	eight	18	eighteen	100	one hundred
9	nine	19	nineteen		
10	ten	20	twenty		

Write the number and number words.

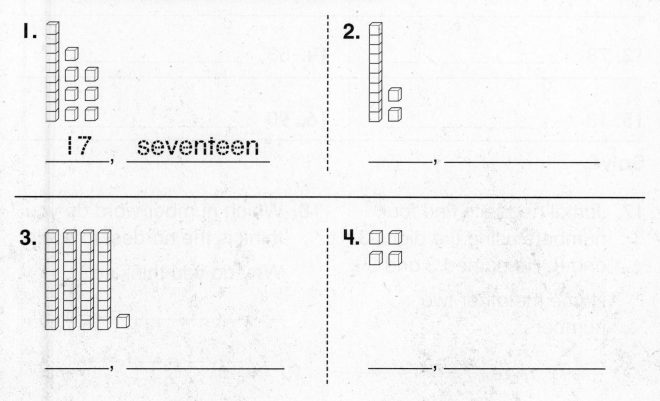

1. ___17___, ___seventeen___

2. _____, _____

3. _____, _____

4. _____, _____

Name _____

Skills Practice

Read and Write Numbers

Write the number or the number words.

1. seventy ___70___   2. sixteen _____

3. thirty-seven _____   4. twenty-five _____

5. eighty-nine _____   6. twelve _____

7. forty-eight _____   8. ninety-two _____

9. fifty-one _____   10. sixty-three _____

11. 23 _____   12. 45 _____

13. 78 _____   14. 53 _____

15. 13 _____   16. 90 _____

Solve.

17. Jamal needs to find four numbers using the digits 3 and 4. He named 3 and 34.

    Name the other two numbers.

    _____

    _____

18. Which number word do you think is the hardest to spell?

    Why do you think so?

    _____

    _____

Name _____

Reteach

Estimate Amounts

Count to get an exact number.

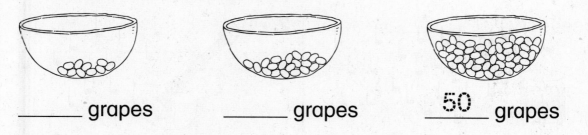

_____ grapes   _____ grapes   50 grapes

**Make your estimate. Use the jars to help.
Circle your answer.**

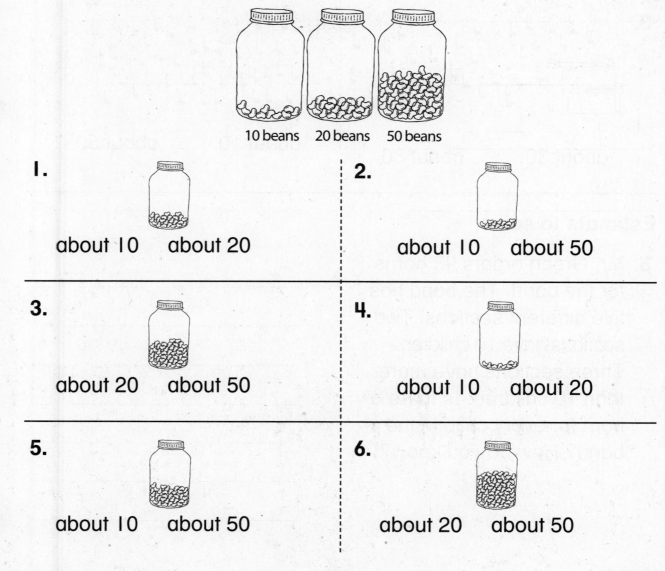

10 beans   20 beans   50 beans

I.
about 10   about 20

2.
about 10   about 50

3.
about 20   about 50

4.
about 10   about 20

5.
about 10   about 50

6.
about 20   about 50

Name _____

Skills Practice

Estimate Amounts

Estimate. Circle your answer.

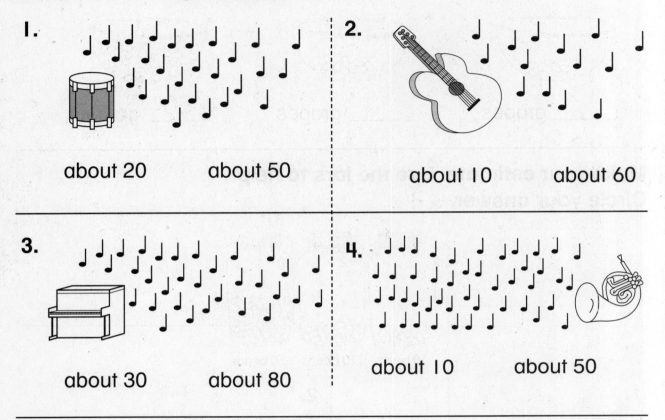

1.
about 20   about 50

2.
about 10   about 60

3.
about 30   about 80

4.
about 10   about 50

Estimate to solve.

5. Mr. Green orders 48 horns for the band. The band has five different sections. Two sections have 10 children. Three sections have more than 10 children. Is there a horn for every child in the band? How do you know?

_____

_____

_____

_____

_____

_____

_____

Name _____

Reteach

Order Numbers

**The hundred chart gives the numbers
1 to 100 in order.**

1	2	3	4	5	6	7	8	9	10
11	12	13	14	15	16	17	18	19	20
21	22	23	24	25	26	27	28	29	30
31	32	33	34	35	36	37	38	39	40
41	42	43	44	45	46	47	48	49	50
51	52	53	54	55	56	57	58	59	60
61	62	63	64	65	66	67	68	69	70
71	72	73	74	75	76	77	78	79	80
81	82	83	84	85	86	87	88	89	90
91	92	93	94	95	96	97	98	99	100

__22__ comes just *before* 23

__25__ comes *between* 24 and 26

__29__ comes just *after* 28

**Use the chart to help you answer.
Write the number that comes:**

just before	just after	between
1. __42__ 43	49, __50__	43, __44__ 45
2. _____ 45	51, _____	47, _____ 49
3. _____ 71	72, _____	74, _____ 76
4. _____ 77	88, _____	90, _____ 92

Circle the correct words.

5. 26 comes _____ 27.

just before

just after

between

6. 28 comes _____ 27.

just before

just after

between

Name _____

Skills Practice

Order Numbers

```
←─┼──┼──┼──┼──┼──┼──┼──┼──┼──┼──┼──┼──┼──┼──┼──┼──┼──┼──┼──┼──┼─→
  30 31 32 33 34 35 36 37 38 39 40 41 42 43 44 45 46 47 48 49 50
```

Use the number line to fill in the blanks.

1. ___33___, 34, 35   43, _____, 45   34, 35, _____

2. _____, 39, 40   45, 46, _____   37, _____, 39

3. 39, _____, 41   47, 48, _____   _____, 46, 47

4. 48, 49, _____   29, _____, 31   _____, 38, 39

5. _____, 38, 39, _____   _____, 31, 32, _____

6. _____, 44, _____, 46   40, _____, _____, 43

7. 37, 38, _____, _____   _____, 39, _____, 41

8. 46, _____, _____, 49   34, 35, _____, _____

Use number order to solve.

9. Cindy drops her notebook.
She picked up pages 28, 29,
32, 33, 34, and 35.

Which pages are missing?

_____

Reteach

Compare Numbers

You can use models to help you compare numbers.
First compare tens. If they are equal, compare ones.

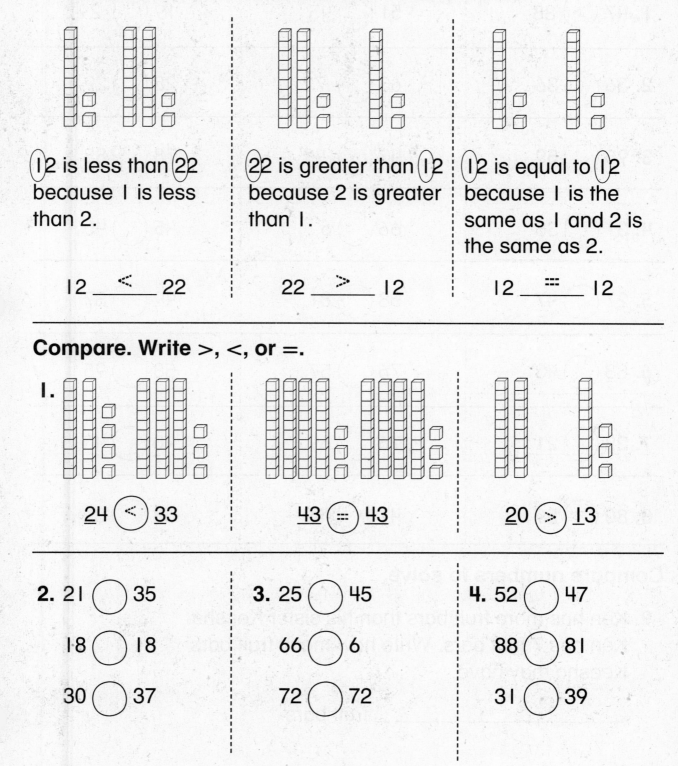

(1)2 is less than (2)2
because 1 is less
than 2.

12 ___<___ 22

(2)2 is greater than (1)2
because 2 is greater
than 1.

22 ___>___ 12

(1)2 is equal to (1)2
because 1 is the
same as 1 and 2 is
the same as 2.

12 ___=___ 12

Compare. Write >, <, or =.

1.

24 (<) 33

43 (=) 43

20 (>) 13

2. 21 ◯ 35

18 ◯ 18

30 ◯ 37

3. 25 ◯ 45

66 ◯ 6

72 ◯ 72

4. 52 ◯ 47

88 ◯ 81

31 ◯ 39

Name _____

Skills Practice

Compare Numbers

Compare. Write >, <, or =.

1. 47 ⊖> 38	51 ◯ 45	19 ◯ 29
2. 36 ◯ 36	63 ◯ 72	23 ◯ 29
3. 95 ◯ 59	43 ◯ 49	78 ◯ 83
4. 31 ◯ 38	66 ◯ 6	45 ◯ 45
5. 27 ◯ 47	58 ◯ 81	49 ◯ 37
6. 83 ◯ 43	76 ◯ 57	58 ◯ 95
7. 28 ◯ 21	76 ◯ 69	40 ◯ 40
8. 80 ◯ 59	47 ◯ 59	68 ◯ 89

Compare numbers to solve.

9. Ken has more fruit bars than his sister Keesha.
Ken has 7 fruit bars. Write how many fruit bars
Keesha may have.

_____ fruit bars

Name _____

Reteach

Patterns

You can use patterns to solve problems.
Some patterns are *repeating patterns*.

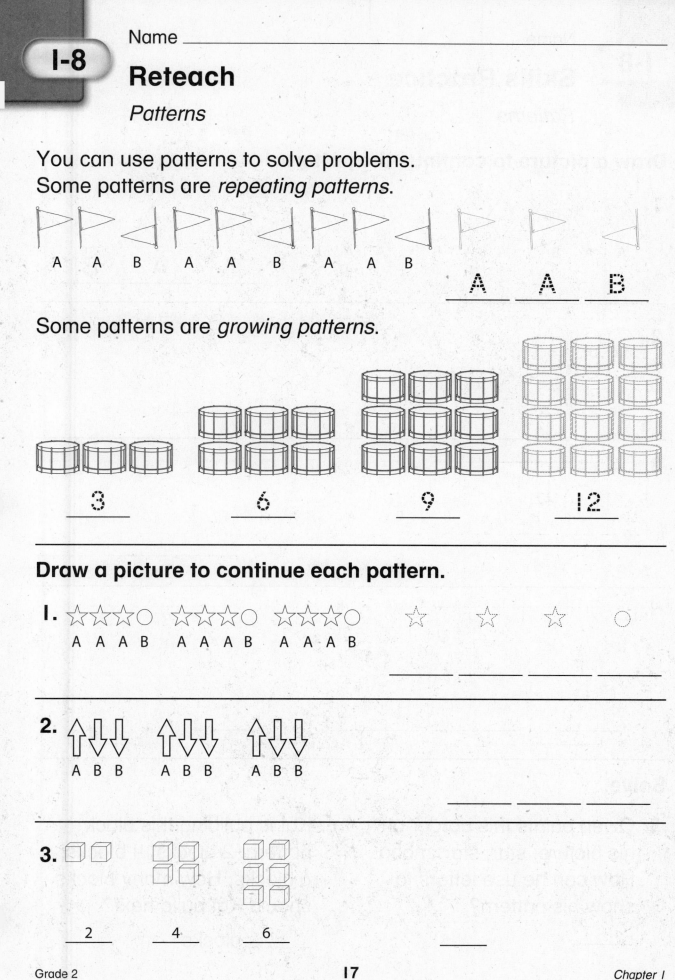

A A B A A B A A B   A   A   B

Some patterns are *growing patterns*.

3   6   9   12

Draw a picture to continue each pattern.

1. ☆☆☆◯ ☆☆☆◯ ☆☆☆◯   ☆   ☆   ☆   ◯
A A A B   A A A B   A A A B

____ ____ ____ ____

---

2. ⬆⬇⬇ ⬆⬇⬇ ⬆⬇⬇
A B B   A B B   A B B

____ ____ ____

---

3. ▢▢   ▢▢   ▢▢
              ▢▢   ▢▢

2   4   6   ____

Name _____

Skills Practice

Patterns

Draw a picture to continue the pattern.

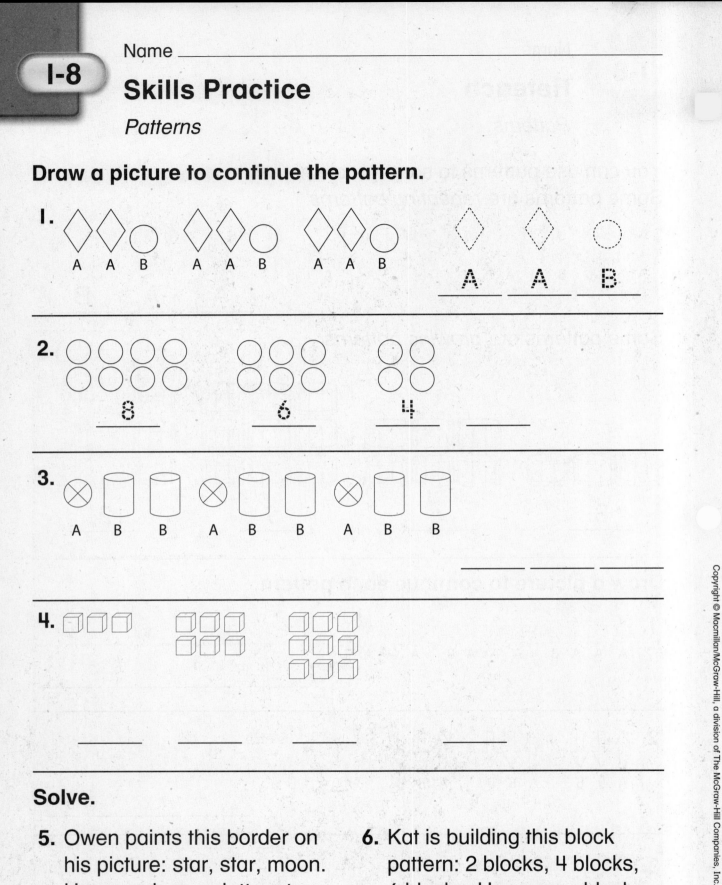

1.

◇ ◇ ○ ◇ ◇ ○ ◇ ◇ ○   ◇   ◇   ○
A A B A A B A A B   A   A   B

2.

8   6   4   ___

3.

A B B A B B A B B   ___ ___ ___

4.

___ ___ ___ ___

Solve.

5. Owen paints this border on his picture: star, star, moon. How can he use letters to show his pattern?

_____

6. Kat is building this block pattern: 2 blocks, 4 blocks, 6 blocks. How many blocks should Kat build next?

_____ blocks

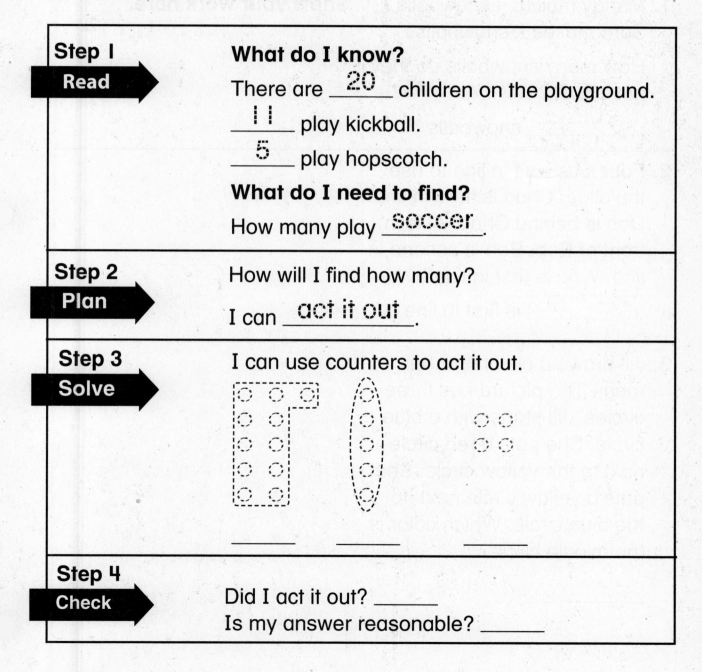

Name _____

Reteach (1)

Problem-Solving Investigation: Choose a Strategy

There are 20 children on the playground.
Eleven children play kickball.
Five children play hopscotch.
The rest play soccer.

How many children play soccer?

Step 1 **Read**	**What do I know?** There are ___20___ children on the playground. ___11___ play kickball. ___5___ play hopscotch. **What do I need to find?** How many play ___soccer___.
Step 2 **Plan**	How will I find how many? I can ___act it out___.
Step 3 **Solve**	I can use counters to act it out. _____ _____ _____
Step 4 **Check**	Did I act it out? _____ Is my answer reasonable? _____

Name _____

Reteach (2)

Problem-Solving Investigation: Choose a Strategy

Choose a strategy and solve.

Problem-Solving Strategies
Draw a picture
Logical reasoning
Act it out

1. Mandy makes 4 snowballs. Sara makes 2 snowballs.

   How many snowballs do they have in all?

   _____ snowballs

   Show your work here.

2. Four kids wait in line to use the slide. Chad is third in line. Don is behind Chad. Al is in front of Bob. Bob is second in line. Who is first in line?

   _____ is first in line.

3. Jill draws a picture for her mom. The picture has three circles. Jill starts with a blue circle. She puts a red circle next to the yellow circle. She puts a yellow circle next to the blue circle. Which color is the middle circle?

   _____

Name _____

Skills Practice

Problem-Solving Investigation: Choose a Strategy

Choose a strategy and solve.

Problem-Solving Strategies
Draw a picture
Logical reasoning
Act it out

1. Kyra is feeding 8 ducks. 5 ducks swim away. How many ducks are left for Kyra to feed?

   _____ ducks are left

Show your work here.

2. Dex does a silly walk. His walk is step, hop, hop, step, hop, hop. How could Dex use A's and B's to show the pattern of his silly walk?

   _____

3. Three children are in line to play kickball. Kim is not second. Cedric will kick after Bob. Bob is not first. In what order will they kick?

   _____

Name _____

Reteach

Patterns on a Hundred Chart

Skip counting on a hundred chart makes patterns.

What is the pattern shown? _____

1	2	3	4	5	6	7	8	9	10
11	12	13	14	15	16	17	18	19	20
21	22	23	24	25	26	27	28	29	30
31	32	33	34	35	36	37	38	39	40
41	42	43	44	45	46	47	48	49	50
51	52	53	54	55	56	57	58	59	60
61	62	63	64	65	66	67	68	69	70
71	72	73	74	75	76	77	78	79	80
81	82	83	84	85	86	87	88	89	90
91	92	93	94	95	96	97	98	99	100

Use a hundred chart to skip count.

1. Start at 1. Skip count by 4. Color.

2. Start at 1. Skip count by 5. Color a different color.

3. Tell what patterns you see in the chart.

_____

_____

_____

1	2	3	4	5	6	7	8	9	10
11	12	13	14	15	16	17	18	19	20
21	22	23	24	25	26	27	28	29	30
31	32	33	34	35	36	37	38	39	40
41	42	43	44	45	46	47	48	49	50
51	52	53	54	55	56	57	58	59	60
61	62	63	64	65	66	67	68	69	70
71	72	73	74	75	76	77	78	79	80
81	82	83	84	85	86	87	88	89	90
91	92	93	94	95	96	97	98	99	100

1-10

Skills Practice

Patterns on a Hundred Chart

Use the hundred chart to skip count.

1	2	3	4	5	6	7	8	9	10
11	12	13	14	15	16	17	18	19	20
21	22	23	24	25	26	27	28	29	30
31	32	33	34	35	36	37	38	39	40
41	42	43	44	45	46	47	48	49	50
51	52	53	54	55	56	57	58	59	60
61	62	63	64	65	66	67	68	69	70
71	72	73	74	75	76	77	78	79	80
81	82	83	84	85	86	87	88	89	90
91	92	93	94	95	96	97	98	99	100

1. Skip count by 3s.

30, 33, 36, _____, _____, _____,

_____.

2. Skip count by 6s.

24, 30, 36, _____, _____, _____,

_____.

3. Skip count by 9s.

18, 27, 36, _____, _____, _____, _____.

Use a number pattern to solve.

4. Clint has to make shoes for 16 horses. How many shoes will he make?

_____

5. Kayla sees seven spiders in her garden. Each spider has 8 legs.

How many legs does she see?

_____

6. Erika has to name the pattern on the number chart.

What should Erika call this pattern?

_____

1	2	3	4	5	6	7	8	9	10
11	12	13	14	15	16	17	18	19	20
21	22	23	24	25	26	27	28	29	30
31	32	33	34	35	36	37	38	39	40
41	42	43	44	45	46	47	48	49	50
51	52	53	54	55	56	57	58	59	60
61	62	63	64	65	66	67	68	69	70
71	72	73	74	75	76	77	78	79	80
81	82	83	84	85	86	87	88	89	90
91	92	93	94	95	96	97	98	99	100

Name _____

Reteach

Addition Properties

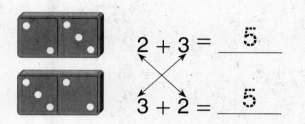

$2 + 3 = \underline{5}$

$3 + 2 = \underline{5}$

The order of the addends is changed. The sum is the same.

$4 + 0 = \underline{4}$

$0 + 4 = \underline{4}$

Add 0 to a number. The sum is the same as the other addend.

Find each sum.

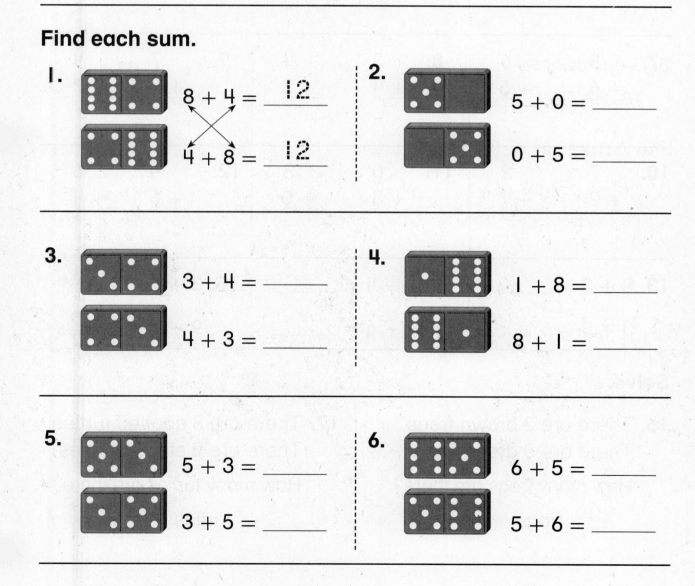

1.

$8 + 4 = \underline{12}$

$4 + 8 = \underline{12}$

2.

$5 + 0 = \underline{}$

$0 + 5 = \underline{}$

3.

$3 + 4 = \underline{}$

$4 + 3 = \underline{}$

4.

$1 + 8 = \underline{}$

$8 + 1 = \underline{}$

5.

$5 + 3 = \underline{}$

$3 + 5 = \underline{}$

6.

$6 + 5 = \underline{}$

$5 + 6 = \underline{}$

25

Name _____

Skills Practice

Addition Properties

Find each sum.

1. 3   2
    +2   +3
    5

2. 5   7
    +7   +5

3. 2   0
    +0   +2

4. 4   5
    +5   +4

5. 7   0
    +0   +7

6. 4   2
    +2   +4

7. 5   6
    +6   +5

8. 3   4
    +4   +3

9. 7   4
    +4   +7

10. 7   2
     +2   +7

11. 0   3
     +3   +0

12. 4   6
     +6   +4

13. $8 + 3 =$ _____

    $3 + 8 =$ _____

14. $6 + 4 =$ _____

    $4 + 6 =$ _____

15. $3 + 9 =$ _____

    $9 + 3 =$ _____

Solve.

16. There are 2 brown frogs.
    There are 8 green frogs.

    How many frogs are there?

    _____ frogs

17. There are 8 spotted turtles.
    There are 2 striped turtles.

    How many turtles are there?

    _____ turtles

Name _____

Reteach

Count On to Add

You can use squares to count on.

Find 5 + 3. Start at 5. Count on 3.

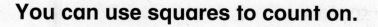

1 2 3 4 5 6 7 8

$5 + 3 = \underline{8}$

$$\begin{array}{r} 5 \\ + 3 \\ \hline 8 \end{array}$$

Use the squares. Add squares to count on.

1. $8 + 1 = \underline{9}$

2. $6 + 2 = \underline{}$

3. $7 + 3 = \underline{}$

4. $5 + 1 = \underline{}$

5. $9 + 3 = \underline{}$

6. $7 + 2 = \underline{}$

7. $6 + 3 = \underline{}$

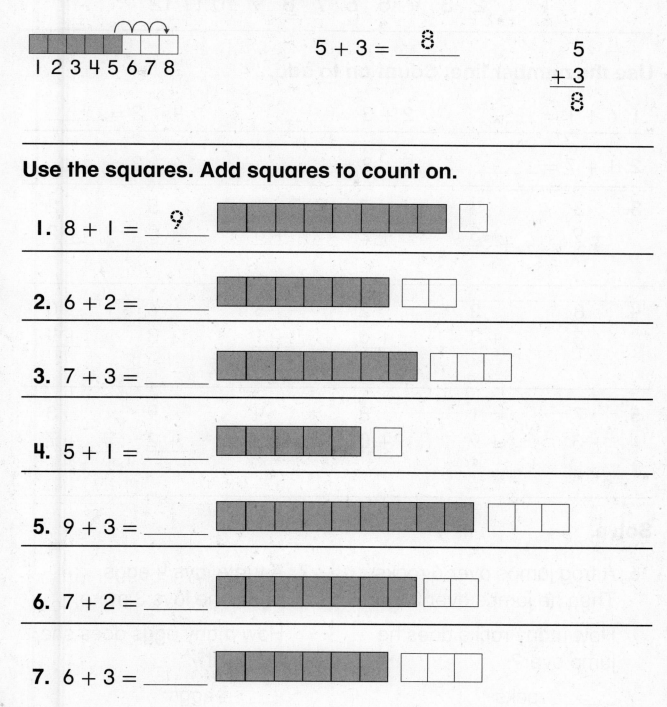

2-2

Skills Practice

Count On to Add

You can use a number line to add.

```
<---+---+---+---+---+---+---+---+---+---+---+---+---+--->
    0   1   2   3   4   5   6   7   8   9   10  11  12
```

Use the number line. Count on to add.

1. $6 + 1 = \underline{\quad 7 \quad}$ $2 + 3 = \underline{\qquad}$ $4 + 3 = \underline{\qquad}$

2. $1 + 7 = \underline{\qquad}$ $5 + 2 = \underline{\qquad}$ $6 + 3 = \underline{\qquad}$

3.
$$\begin{array}{cccccc} 3 & 4 & 7 & 1 & 5 & 2 \\ +9 & +3 & +2 & +6 & +0 & +2 \end{array}$$

4.
$$\begin{array}{cccccc} 8 & 2 & 2 & 5 & 6 & 0 \\ +3 & +3 & +6 & +1 & +3 & +4 \end{array}$$

5.
$$\begin{array}{cccccc} 7 & 1 & 8 & 4 & 9 & 3 \\ +3 & +9 & +0 & +2 & +2 & +7 \end{array}$$

Solve.

6. A frog jumps over 6 rocks. Then he jumps over 2 more.

How many rocks does he jump over?

_____ rocks

7. A turtle lays 4 eggs. Then she lays 3 more.

How many eggs does she lay in all?

_____ eggs

Name _____

Reteach (1)

Problem-Solving Strategy: Act It Out

Jeff likes to watch birds on the way to school. Today, he saw 5 crows and 12 robins. How many birds did Jeff see?

Step 1
Understand ▶

What do I know?
 Jeff saw 5 crows.
 Jeff saw 12 robins.

What do I need to find out?
 How many birds did Jeff see?

Step 2
Plan ▶

How will I find how many birds he saw?

 I can act it out using _____.

Step 3
Solve ▶

Act it out
 I can use red counters to stand for robins.
 I can use white counters for crows.

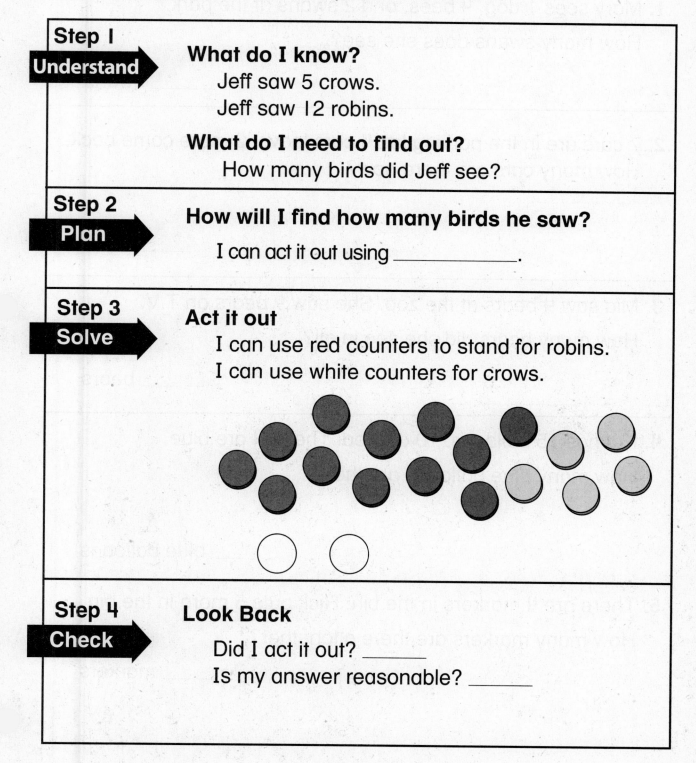

Step 4
Check ▶

Look Back
 Did I act it out? _____
 Is my answer reasonable? _____

Name _____

Reteach (2)

Problem-Solving Strategy: Act It Out

Solve. Use counters to act it out.

1. Mary sees 1 dog, 4 bees, and 2 swans at the park.

How many swans does she see?

_____ swans

2. 7 cars are in the parking lot. 4 cars leave. 2 more come back.
How many cars are there now?

_____ cars

3. Mia saw 4 bears at the zoo. She saw 9 bears on T.V.

How many bears did she see in all?

_____ bears

4. Kat has 15 balloons. 10 are red. The rest are blue.
How many blue balloons are there?

_____ blue balloons

5. There are 4 markers in the bin. Rick puts 5 more in the bin.

How many markers are there altogether?

_____ markers

Name _____

Skills Practice

Problem-Solving Strategy: Act It Out

Solve. Use classroom erasers to act it out.

1. Scott buys all the  and  erasers.

   How many erasers does he buy in all? _____

2. Kelly buys all the  erasers.

   How many erasers does she have? _____

3. Sara buys all the  erasers. Then she buys all the  erasers.

   How many erasers does she have? _____

4. Ted buys all the  and  erasers. Then he buys 8 more erasers.

   How many erasers does he have? _____

Reteach

Doubles

Addends that are the same are called doubles.

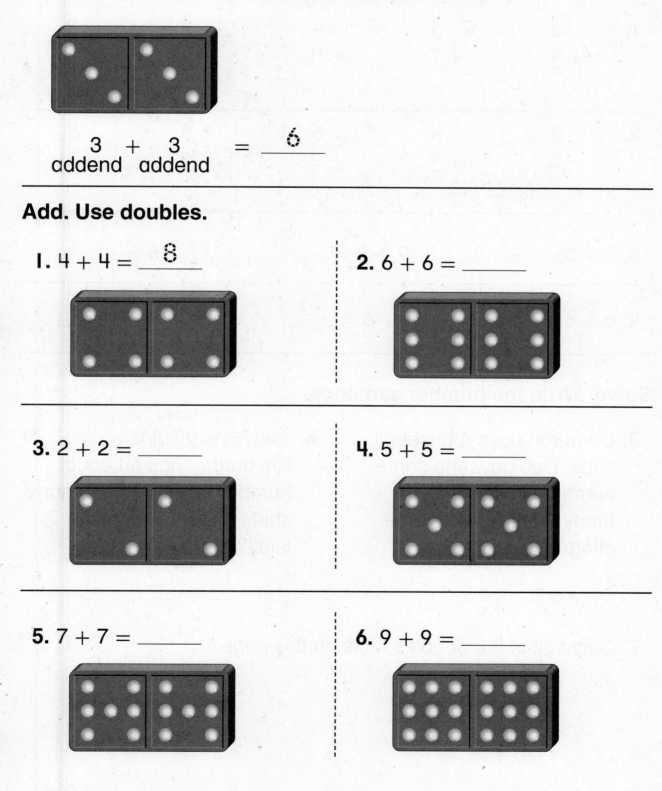

$$3 + 3 = \underline{6}$$
addend addend

Add. Use doubles.

1. $4 + 4 = \underline{8}$

2. $6 + 6 = \underline{}$

---

3. $2 + 2 = \underline{}$

4. $5 + 5 = \underline{}$

---

5. $7 + 7 = \underline{}$

6. $9 + 9 = \underline{}$

Name _____

Skills Practice

Doubles

Add.

1.
$$\begin{array}{r} 3 \\ +4 \\ \hline \end{array} \qquad \begin{array}{r} 5 \\ +7 \\ \hline \end{array} \qquad \begin{array}{r} 4 \\ +4 \\ \hline \end{array} \qquad \begin{array}{r} 8 \\ +4 \\ \hline \end{array} \qquad \begin{array}{r} 9 \\ +0 \\ \hline \end{array}$$

2.
$$\begin{array}{r} 3 \\ +3 \\ \hline \end{array} \qquad \begin{array}{r} 4 \\ +9 \\ \hline \end{array} \qquad \begin{array}{r} 6 \\ +2 \\ \hline \end{array} \qquad \begin{array}{r} 8 \\ +8 \\ \hline \end{array} \qquad \begin{array}{r} 6 \\ +7 \\ \hline \end{array}$$

3. $8 + 3 =$ _____ $9 + 9 =$ _____ $7 + 6 =$ _____

4. $6 + 6 =$ _____ $7 + 6 =$ _____ $7 + 7 =$ _____

Solve. Write the number sentence.

5. Cameron buys 6 baseball caps. Deb buys the same number of caps. How many caps do they have altogether?

_____ + _____ = _____

6. Andy has 9 shirts. His brother has an equal number of shirts. How many shirts do the boys have in all?

_____ + _____ = _____

7. Circle all of the doubles facts on this page.

Name _____

Reteach

Near Doubles

Knowing doubles can help you learn other facts.

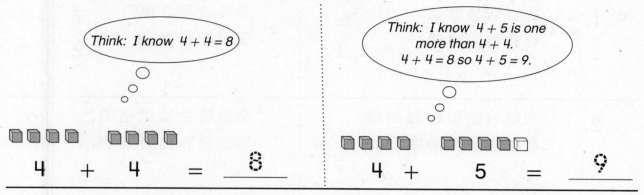

Think: I know $4 + 4 = 8$

$4 + 4 = $ ___8___

Think: I know $4 + 5$ is one more than $4 + 4$.
$4 + 4 = 8$ so $4 + 5 = 9$.

$4 + 5 = $ ___9___

Find the sum. Use doubles to help.

1.

$4 + 4 = $ ___8___

$4 + 5 = $ _____

2.

$6 + 6 = $ _____

$6 + 5 = $ _____

3.
$\begin{array}{r} 5 \\ + 5 \\ \hline \end{array}$ $\qquad$ $\begin{array}{r} 5 \\ + 6 \\ \hline \end{array}$

4.
$\begin{array}{r} 8 \\ + 8 \\ \hline \end{array}$ $\qquad$ $\begin{array}{r} 8 \\ + 9 \\ \hline \end{array}$

5.
$\begin{array}{r} 6 \\ + 6 \\ \hline \end{array}$ $\qquad$ $\begin{array}{r} 6 \\ + 7 \\ \hline \end{array}$

6.
$\begin{array}{r} 8 \\ + 8 \\ \hline \end{array}$ $\qquad$ $\begin{array}{r} 8 \\ + 7 \\ \hline \end{array}$

7.
$\begin{array}{r} 10 \\ + 10 \\ \hline \end{array}$ $\qquad$ $\begin{array}{r} 10 \\ + 9 \\ \hline \end{array}$

8.
$\begin{array}{r} 7 \\ + 7 \\ \hline \end{array}$ $\qquad$ $\begin{array}{r} 7 \\ + 8 \\ \hline \end{array}$

Name _____

Skills Practice

Near Doubles

Find the sum. Use near doubles to help.

1. $\begin{array}{r} 6 \\ + 6 \\ \hline \end{array}$ $\quad\quad$ $\begin{array}{r} 7 \\ + 6 \\ \hline \end{array}$

2. $\begin{array}{r} 9 \\ + 9 \\ \hline \end{array}$ $\quad\quad$ $\begin{array}{r} 9 \\ + 8 \\ \hline \end{array}$

Find the sum. Use doubles and near doubles to help.

3.

$7 + 7 = $ ____	
one less	one more
$7 + 6 = $ ___	$7 + 8 = $ ____

4.

$5 + 5 = $ ____	
one less	one more
$5 + 4 = $ ___	$5 + 6 = $ ____

5.

$6 + 6 = $ ____	
one less	one more
$6 + 5 = $ ___	$6 + 7 = $ ____

6.

$9 + 9 = $ ____	
one less	one more
$9 + 8 = $ ___	$9 + 10 = $ ___

7. Annie sees 4 bullfrogs at the lake. Zack sees 1 less bullfrog than Annie. Write an addition sentence that tells how many bullfrogs they saw.

____ + ____ = ____ bullfrogs

8. Marcy finds 5 ladybugs. Lee finds 1 more ladybug than Marcy. Write an addition sentence that tells how many ladybugs they found.

____ + ____ = ____ ladybugs

Name _____

Reteach

Make a 10

You can make a 10 to help you add. **Move 1 to make a 10.**

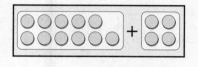

9 + 4

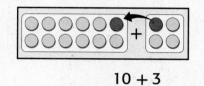

10 + 3

Now add 10 + 3.

$$10 + 3 = 13$$
$$9 + 4 = 13$$

Add. Color the counters you use to make a 10.

1.   7 ⎫ can be changed to   ___10___
        + 6 ⎭   + 3
                                      _____

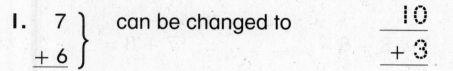

2.   8 ⎫ can be changed to   ___10___
        + 3 ⎭   + 1
                                      _____

3. 6 + 9 = ____   ____ + 10 = ____

4. 8 + 6 = ____   10 + ____ = ____

Name _____

Skills Practice

Make a 10

Add. Use connecting cubes to help.

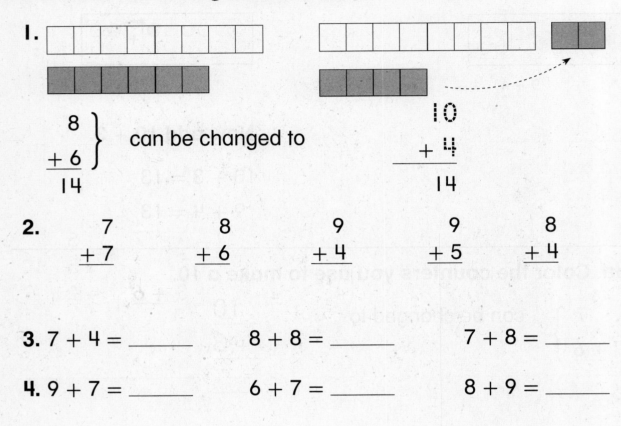

1.

$$\left.\begin{array}{r} 8 \\ + 6 \\ \hline 14 \end{array}\right\}$$ can be changed to $$\begin{array}{r} 10 \\ + 4 \\ \hline 14 \end{array}$$

2.
$$\begin{array}{r} 7 \\ + 7 \\ \hline \end{array} \qquad \begin{array}{r} 8 \\ + 6 \\ \hline \end{array} \qquad \begin{array}{r} 9 \\ + 4 \\ \hline \end{array} \qquad \begin{array}{r} 9 \\ + 5 \\ \hline \end{array} \qquad \begin{array}{r} 8 \\ + 4 \\ \hline \end{array}$$

3. 7 + 4 = _____   8 + 8 = _____   7 + 8 = _____

4. 9 + 7 = _____   6 + 7 = _____   8 + 9 = _____

Solve.

5. Ali built 8 model airplanes in October. In November she built 6 model airplanes.

   How many airplanes has she built in all?

   __8__ + _____   _____.

6. Marty learned to play 7 new songs in January. In February, he learned 5 new songs.

   How many songs has he learned in the two months?

   _____ + _____   _____

Name _____

Reteach

Add Three Numbers

You can group addends.
You can use doubles or
make a 10.

Find a double.

$$\begin{matrix} 4 \\ 3 \end{matrix} \Big\rangle 8 \\ +4 \quad +3 \\ \hline \quad 11$$

Make a 10.

$$\begin{matrix} 6 \\ 5 \end{matrix} \Big\rangle 10 \\ +4 \quad +5 \\ \hline \quad 15$$

Find a double. Circle addends that make doubles. Add.

1. $\begin{matrix} 3 \\ 3 \end{matrix} \diagdown \boxed{6} \\ +7 \quad +7 \\ \hline \qquad 13$

$\begin{matrix} 4 \\ 2 \\ +2 \end{matrix}$ $\begin{matrix} 4 \\ 4 \\ + \end{matrix}$ $\begin{matrix} 4 \\ 5 \\ +4 \end{matrix}$ $\begin{matrix} 5 \\ \\ +8 \end{matrix}$ $\begin{matrix} 3 \\ 7 \\ +3 \end{matrix}$ $\begin{matrix} 7 \\ \\ +6 \end{matrix}$ $\begin{matrix} 5 \\ 5 \\ +2 \end{matrix}$ $\begin{matrix} \\ 10 \\ +2 \end{matrix}$

Make a 10. Circle addends that make a 10. Add.

2. $\begin{matrix} 8 \\ 2 \end{matrix} \diagup \boxed{10} \\ +4 \quad +4 \\ \hline \qquad 14$

$\begin{matrix} 4 \\ 3 \\ +6 \end{matrix}$ $\begin{matrix} 3 \\ \\ + \end{matrix} 10$ $\begin{matrix} 1 \\ 9 \\ +4 \end{matrix}$ $\begin{matrix} \\ 10 \\ +4 \end{matrix}$ $\begin{matrix} 8 \\ 7 \\ +3 \end{matrix}$ $\begin{matrix} 8 \\ 10 \\ + \end{matrix}$ $\begin{matrix} 5 \\ 6 \\ +5 \end{matrix}$ $\begin{matrix} 6 \\ 10 \\ + \end{matrix}$

Find the sum.

3. $\begin{matrix} 8 \\ 3 \end{matrix} \diagdown \begin{matrix} \\ 3 \end{matrix} \\ +8 \quad +16$

$\begin{matrix} 8 \\ 9 \\ +1 \end{matrix} \diagup \begin{matrix} \\ 8 \\ +10 \end{matrix}$

$\begin{matrix} 9 \\ 9 \end{matrix} \diagdown 18 \\ +2 \quad +2$

$\begin{matrix} 2 \\ 7 \end{matrix} \diagdown \begin{matrix} \\ 7 \end{matrix} \\ +8 \quad +10$

$\begin{matrix} 8 \\ 0 \end{matrix} \diagdown \begin{matrix} \\ 0 \end{matrix} \\ +8 \quad +16$

Name _____

Skills Practice

Add Three Numbers

Find each sum.

1.

3	4	8	4	5	9
2	5	0	3	4	1
+ 3	+ 4	+ 2	+ 4	+ 6	+ 5
8					

2.

4	7	9	8	7	5
8	6	1	3	3	5
+ 2	+ 6	+ 4	+ 8	+ 6	+ 5

3.

4	3	0	2	8	3
6	5	7	4	2	6
+ 8	+ 3	+ 7	+ 8	+ 3	+ 7

4.

6	4	8	5	1	3
5	4	2	3	9	8
+ 6	+ 7	+ 4	+ 5	+ 6	+ 2

Solve.

5. Jan has 4 stamps. Tim has 9 stamps. Ben has 4 stamps. How many total stamps do they have?

_____ stamps

6. There are 4 bear stickers, 6 wolf stickers, and 8 fox stickers. How many stickers are there in all?

_____ stickers

Name _____

Reteach (1)

Problem-Solving Investigation: Choose a Strategy

Jen: It takes me 10 minutes to clean my room.
It takes me 2 minutes to brush my teeth.
It takes me 5 minutes to change my clothes.
How long will it take me to get ready for bed?

Choose a strategy to solve.

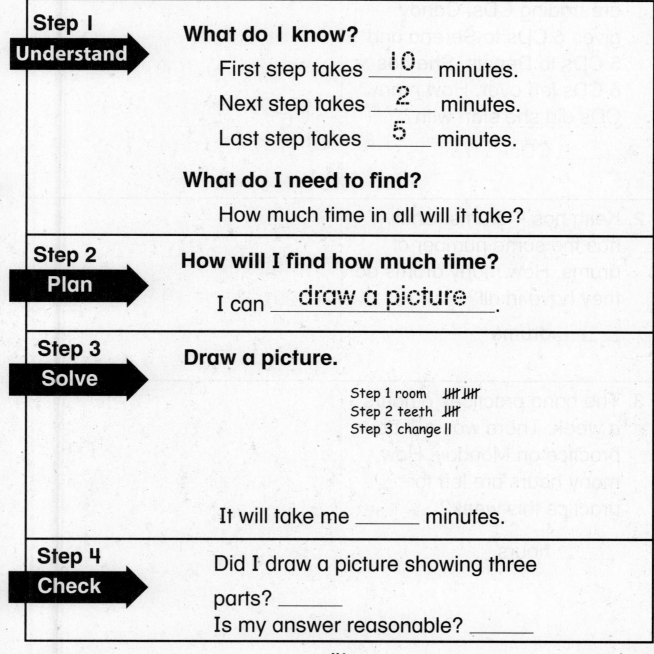

Step 1
Understand

What do I know?

First step takes ____10____ minutes.

Next step takes ____2____ minutes.

Last step takes ____5____ minutes.

What do I need to find?

How much time in all will it take?

Step 2
Plan

How will I find how much time?

I can ____draw a picture____.

Step 3
Solve

Draw a picture.

Step 1 room   卌 卌
Step 2 teeth   卌
Step 3 change ll

It will take me _____ minutes.

Step 4
Check

Did I draw a picture showing three parts? _____
Is my answer reasonable? _____

Reteach (2)

Problem-Solving Investigation: Choose a Strategy

Choose a strategy and solve.

Problem-Solving Strategies
Use logical reasoning
Act it out
Draw a picture

Name _____

1. Candy, Dennis, and Serena are trading CDs. Candy gives 6 CDs to Serena and 5 CDs to Dennis. She has 6 CDs left over. How many CDs did she start with?

_____ CDs

Show your work here.

2. Keith has 4 drums. Shawn has the same number of drums. How many drums do they have in all?

_____ drums

3. The band practices 6 hours a week. There was a 3-hour practice on Monday. How many hours are left to practice this week?

_____ hours

Name _____

Skills Practice

Problem-Solving Investigation: Choose a Strategy

Choose a strategy and solve.

| **Problem-Solving Strategies** |
| Draw a picture |
| Use logical reasoning |
| Act it out |

1. Mrs. Adler washes 4 sweaters on Monday. On Tuesday, Mr. Adler washes 1 less sweater. How many sweaters have the Adlers washed in all?

_____ sweaters

Show your work here.

2. Ken has 2 blue shirts, 3 white shirts, and 7 striped shirts. How many total shirts does he have?

_____ shirts

3. Linda is sewing beads onto her favorite hat. She uses 4 silver beads, 4 clear beads, and 6 gold beads. How many beads in all does Linda use?

_____ beads

43

Name _____

Reteach

Count Back to Subtract

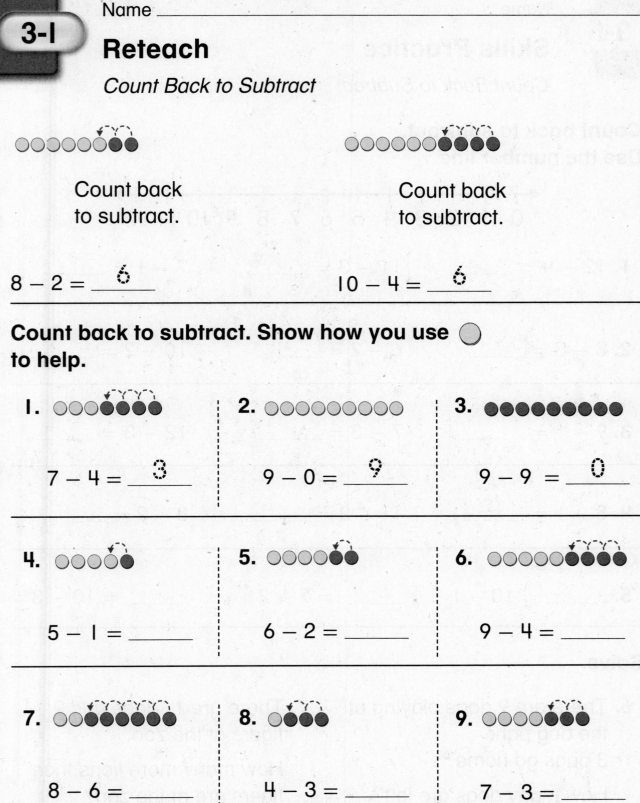

Count back
to subtract.

Count back
to subtract.

$8 - 2 =$ ___6___

$10 - 4 =$ ___6___

Count back to subtract. Show how you use ⚪ to help.

1. $7 - 4 =$ ___3___

2. $9 - 0 =$ ___9___

3. $9 - 9 =$ ___0___

4. $5 - 1 =$ _____

5. $6 - 2 =$ _____

6. $9 - 4 =$ _____

7. $8 - 6 =$ _____

8. $4 - 3 =$ _____

9. $7 - 3 =$ _____

Name _____

Skills Practice

Count Back to Subtract

Count back to subtract.
Use the number line.

```
←|———|———|———|———|———|———|———|———|———|———|———|———|———→
  0   1   2   3   4   5   6   7   8   9   10  11  12
```

1. $12 - 4 =$ _____ $11 - 3 =$ _____ $7 - 1 =$ _____

2. $8 - 3 =$ _____ $6 - 2 =$ _____ $10 - 2 =$ _____

3. $9 - 1 =$ _____ $7 - 3 =$ _____ $12 - 3 =$ _____

4. $8 - 1 =$ _____ $11 - 2 =$ _____ $8 - 2 =$ _____

5. _____ $= 10 - 1$ _____ $= 7 - 2$ _____ $= 10 - 3$

Solve.

6. There are 9 dogs playing at the dog park.
3 dogs go home.

How many dogs are left?

_____ dogs

7. There are 11 lions and 2 tigers at the zoo.

How many more lions than tigers are at the zoo?

_____ lions

Name _____

Reteach

Subtract All and Subtract Zero

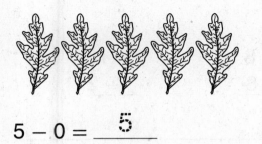

$5 - 0 =$ ___5___

Subtract **0**.
You have the same number left.

$5 - 5 =$ ___0___

Subtract **all**.
You have 0 left.

Subtract. You can cross out pictures to help.

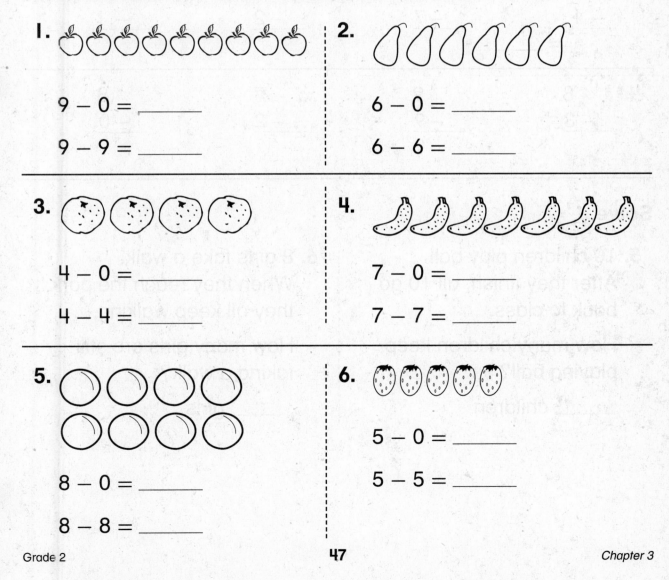

1.

$9 - 0 =$ _____

$9 - 9 =$ _____

2.

$6 - 0 =$ _____

$6 - 6 =$ _____

3.

$4 - 0 =$ _____

$4 - 4 =$ _____

4.

$7 - 0 =$ _____

$7 - 7 =$ _____

5.

$8 - 0 =$ _____

$8 - 8 =$ _____

6.

$5 - 0 =$ _____

$5 - 5 =$ _____

3-2

Skills Practice

Subtract All and Subtract Zero

Subtract.

1. $\begin{array}{r} 7 \\ -1 \\ \hline \end{array}$ $\begin{array}{r} 9 \\ -0 \\ \hline \end{array}$ $\begin{array}{r} 8 \\ -8 \\ \hline \end{array}$ $\begin{array}{r} 10 \\ -2 \\ \hline \end{array}$

2. $\begin{array}{r} 6 \\ -6 \\ \hline \end{array}$ $\begin{array}{r} 9 \\ -3 \\ \hline \end{array}$ $\begin{array}{r} 6 \\ -0 \\ \hline \end{array}$ $\begin{array}{r} 8 \\ -1 \\ \hline \end{array}$

3. $\begin{array}{r} 9 \\ -1 \\ \hline \end{array}$ $\begin{array}{r} 7 \\ -7 \\ \hline \end{array}$ $\begin{array}{r} 9 \\ -2 \\ \hline \end{array}$ $\begin{array}{r} 10 \\ -1 \\ \hline \end{array}$

4. $\begin{array}{r} 8 \\ -3 \\ \hline \end{array}$ $\begin{array}{r} 9 \\ -9 \\ \hline \end{array}$ $\begin{array}{r} 7 \\ -2 \\ \hline \end{array}$ $\begin{array}{r} 8 \\ -0 \\ \hline \end{array}$

Solve.

5. 10 children play ball. After they finish, all 10 go back to class.

   How many children keep playing ball?

   _____ children

6. 8 girls take a walk. When they reach the park, they all keep walking.

   How many girls are still taking a walk?

   _____ girls

3-3

Reteach

Use Doubles to Subtract

You can use doubles facts to subtract.

Remember, doubles are addends that are the same number.

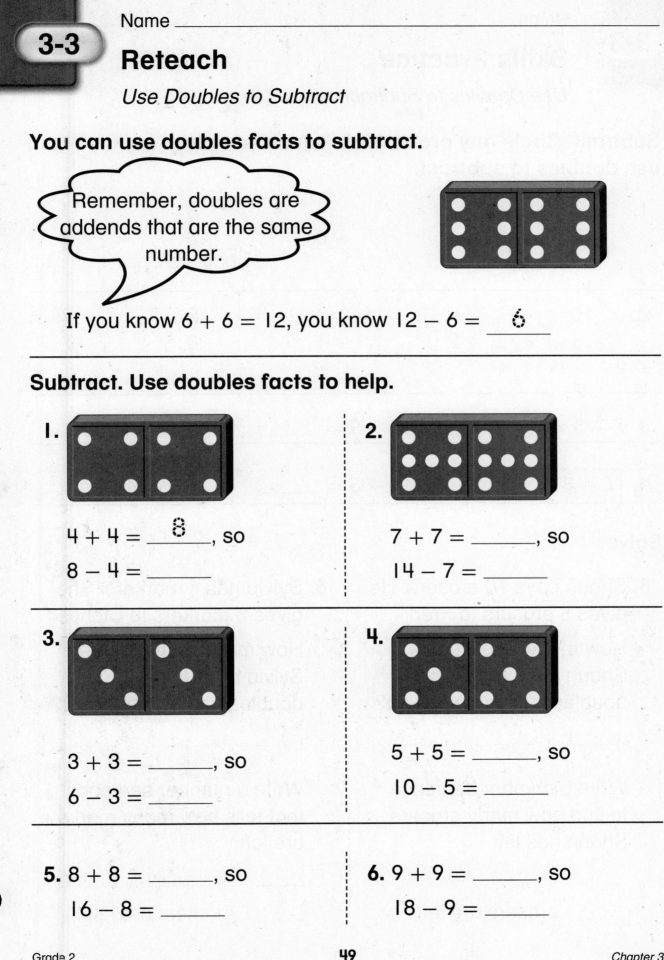

If you know $6 + 6 = 12$, you know $12 - 6 = \underline{6}$

Subtract. Use doubles facts to help.

1. $4 + 4 = \underline{8}$, so

   $8 - 4 = \underline{\hspace{1cm}}$

2. $7 + 7 = \underline{\hspace{1cm}}$, so

   $14 - 7 = \underline{\hspace{1cm}}$

3. $3 + 3 = \underline{\hspace{1cm}}$, so

   $6 - 3 = \underline{\hspace{1cm}}$

4. $5 + 5 = \underline{\hspace{1cm}}$, so

   $10 - 5 = \underline{\hspace{1cm}}$

5. $8 + 8 = \underline{\hspace{1cm}}$, so

   $16 - 8 = \underline{\hspace{1cm}}$

6. $9 + 9 = \underline{\hspace{1cm}}$, so

   $18 - 9 = \underline{\hspace{1cm}}$

Name _____

Skills Practice

Use Doubles to Subtract

Subtract. Circle any problems in which you can use doubles to subtract.

1.

$$
\begin{array}{r} 7 \\ -7 \\ \hline \end{array}
\qquad
\begin{array}{r} 12 \\ -6 \\ \hline \end{array}
\qquad
\begin{array}{r} 4 \\ -0 \\ \hline \end{array}
\qquad
\begin{array}{r} 8 \\ -3 \\ \hline \end{array}
\qquad
\begin{array}{r} 11 \\ -3 \\ \hline \end{array}
$$

2.

$$
\begin{array}{r} 10 \\ -5 \\ \hline \end{array}
\qquad
\begin{array}{r} 4 \\ -2 \\ \hline \end{array}
\qquad
\begin{array}{r} 8 \\ -4 \\ \hline \end{array}
\qquad
\begin{array}{r} 8 \\ -0 \\ \hline \end{array}
\qquad
\begin{array}{r} 7 \\ -7 \\ \hline \end{array}
$$

3. $7 - 3 =$ _____ $18 - 9 =$ _____ $7 - 7 =$ _____

4. $16 - 8 =$ _____ $10 - 3 =$ _____ $14 - 7 =$ _____

Solve.

5. Shaun buys 10 erasers. He gives 5 erasers to Fred.

How many erasers does Shaun have left? What doubles fact can help you?

_____ + _____ = _____

Write a number sentence to find how many erasers Shaun has left.

_____ − _____ = _____

_____ erasers are left

6. Sylvia has 6 markers. She gives 3 markers to Clarice.

How many markers does Sylvia have left? What doubles fact can help you?

_____ + _____ = _____

Write a number sentence that tells how many markers are left.

_____ − _____ = _____

_____ markers are left

50

Name _____

Reteach (1)

Problem-Solving Strategy: Guess and Check

Daryll has 10 pairs of socks in his drawer.
All the socks are either black or white.
There are 4 more pairs of white socks than black socks.
How many pairs of each color socks are there?

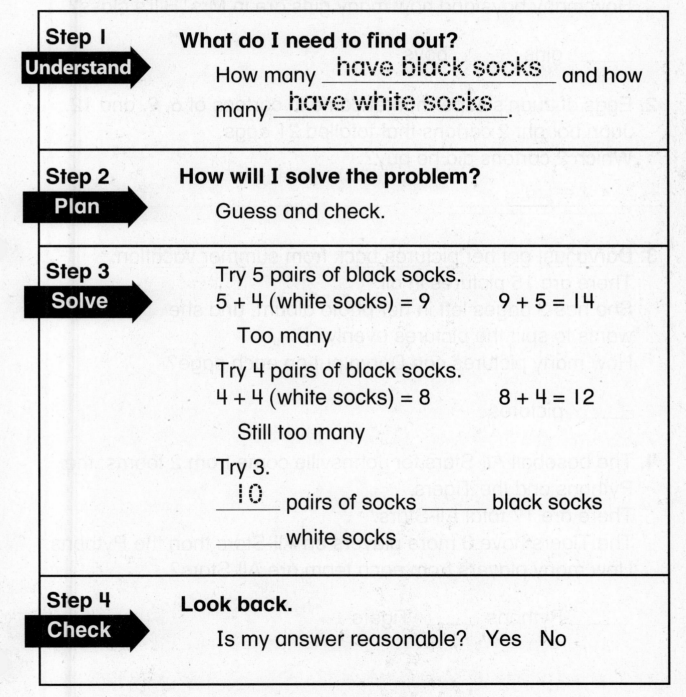

Step 1
Understand

What do I need to find out?

How many ___have black socks___ and how
many ___have white socks___.

Step 2
Plan

How will I solve the problem?

Guess and check.

Step 3
Solve

Try 5 pairs of black socks.
5 + 4 (white socks) = 9   9 + 5 = 14
  Too many

Try 4 pairs of black socks.
4 + 4 (white socks) = 8   8 + 4 = 12
  Still too many

Try 3.
___10___ pairs of socks _____ black socks

_____ white socks

Step 4
Check

Look back.

Is my answer reasonable? Yes No

Name _____

Reteach (2)

Problem-Solving Strategy: Guess and Check

Guess and check.

1. There are 15 students in Mrs. Hill's English Class.
   There are 3 more girls than boys.
   How many boys and how many girls are in Mrs. Hill's class?

   _____ girls _____ boys

2. Eggs at Juan's supermarket come in cartons of 6, 9, and 12.
   Juan bought 2 cartons that totalled 21 eggs.
   Which 2 cartons did he buy?

   _____

3. Darva just got her pictures back from summer vacation.
   There are 15 pictures in all.
   She has 3 pages left in her photo album, and she
   wants to split the pictures evenly.
   How many pictures can Darva put on each page?

   _____ pictures

4. The baseball All-Stars for Johnsville come from 2 teams: the
   Pythons and the Tigers.
   There are 17 total All-Stars.
   The Tigers have 3 more players on All-Stars than the Pythons.
   How many players from each team are All-Stars?

   _____ Pythons _____ Tigers

Name _____

Skills Practice

Problem-Solving Strategy: Guess and Check

Guess and check.

1. Mr. Mahan mixes up all the class pens and pencils.
   He tells the students there are 24 pens and pencils in all.
   The he says there are 10 more pencils than pens.
   How many pencils are there in Mr. Mahan's class?

   _____ pencils

2. Erica needs 16 more flowers to finish planting her garden.
   John's Nursery sells flowers in cartons of 4, 9, and 12.
   Erica bought the two cartons that gave her exactly
   the right amount.
   Which size flower cartons did she buy?

   _____

3. Gramma Jones just picked 16 tomatoes from her garden.
   She decided to split the tomatoes evenly among her
   4 grandchildren.
   How many tomatoes does each grandchild get?

   _____ tomatoes

4. 13 students volunteer for the annual toy drive.
   5 more boys volunteer than girls.
   How many boys and girls volunteer?

   _____ boys _____ girls

Reteach

Relate Addition to Subtraction

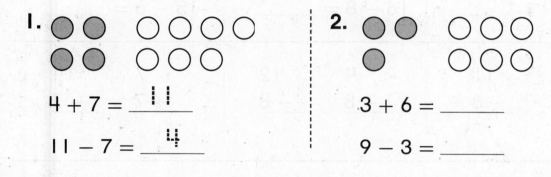

$8 + 4 = \underline{12}$

$12 - 4 = \underline{8}$

These addition and subtraction facts have the same three numbers.

Use addition facts to subtract.

1.

$4 + 7 = \underline{11}$

$11 - 7 = \underline{4}$

2.

$3 + 6 = \underline{}$

$9 - 3 = \underline{}$

3.

$9 + 3 = \underline{}$

$12 - 3 = \underline{}$

4.

$2 + 5 = \underline{}$

$7 - 5 = \underline{}$

5.

$2 + 8 = \underline{}$

$10 - 2 = \underline{}$

6.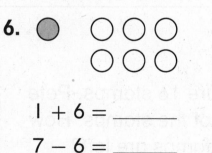

$1 + 6 = \underline{}$

$7 - 6 = \underline{}$

Name _____

Skills Practice

Relate Addition to Subtraction

Use addition facts to subtract.

1. $8 + 5 =$ __13__ | $6 + 8 =$ _____ | $6 + 7 =$ _____
   $13 - 5 =$ _____ | $14 - 8 =$ _____ | $13 - 7 =$ _____

2. $4 + 9 =$ _____ | $8 + 8 =$ _____ | $6 + 9 =$ _____
   $13 - 4 =$ _____ | $16 - 8 =$ _____ | $15 - 6 =$ _____

3.
$$\begin{array}{cc} 3 & 11 \\ +8 & -8 \end{array} \qquad \begin{array}{cc} 4 & 12 \\ +8 & -8 \end{array} \qquad \begin{array}{cc} 7 & 14 \\ +7 & -7 \end{array}$$

4.
$$\begin{array}{cc} 8 & 15 \\ +7 & -8 \end{array} \qquad \begin{array}{cc} 9 & 16 \\ +7 & -9 \end{array} \qquad \begin{array}{cc} 8 & 17 \\ +9 & -8 \end{array}$$

5.
$$\begin{array}{cc} 5 & 14 \\ +9 & -5 \end{array} \qquad \begin{array}{cc} 3 & 12 \\ +9 & -3 \end{array} \qquad \begin{array}{cc} 9 & 18 \\ +9 & -9 \end{array}$$

Solve.

6. There are 16 stamps. Pete uses 8 of the stamps. How many stamps are left?

   _____ stamps

7. Megan writes 4 letters on Monday. She writes 9 letters on Tuesday. How many letters does Megan write?

   _____ letters

Name _____

Reteach

Missing Addends

$9 + \boxed{} = 14$

Related facts use the
same three numbers.

Write a related fact.

$14 - 9 = \underline{5}$,

so, $9 + \underline{5} = 14$.

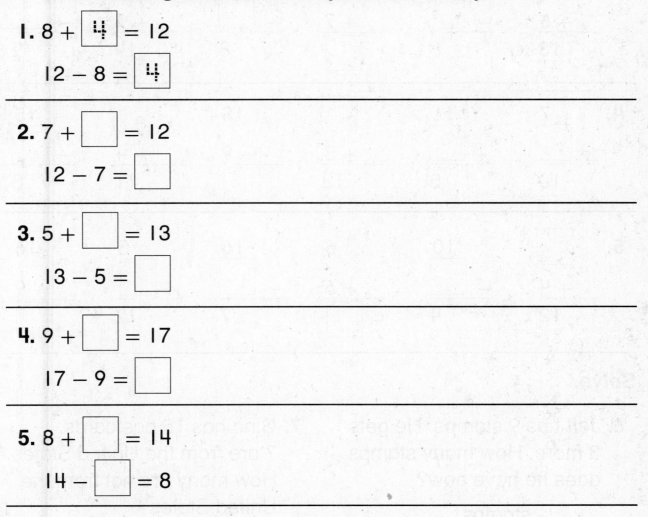

Find the missing addend. Draw pictures to help.

1. $8 + \boxed{4} = 12$

$12 - 8 = \boxed{4}$

---

2. $7 + \boxed{} = 12$

$12 - 7 = \boxed{}$

---

3. $5 + \boxed{} = 13$

$13 - 5 = \boxed{}$

---

4. $9 + \boxed{} = 17$

$17 - 9 = \boxed{}$

---

5. $8 + \boxed{} = 14$

$14 - \boxed{} = 8$

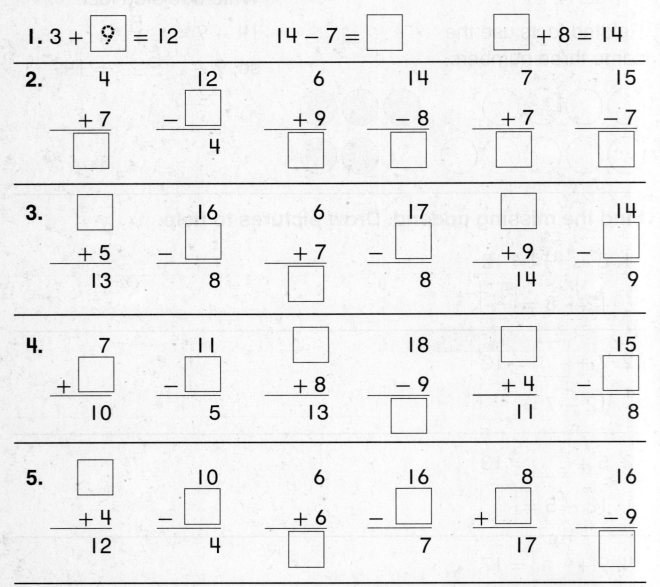

3-6

Skills Practice

Missing Addends

Name _____

Find each missing addend.

1. $3 + \boxed{9} = 12$ $14 - 7 = \boxed{}$ $\boxed{} + 8 = 14$

2.
$\begin{array}{r} 4 \\ +7 \\ \hline \boxed{} \end{array}$
$\begin{array}{r} 12 \\ -\boxed{} \\ \hline 4 \end{array}$
$\begin{array}{r} 6 \\ +9 \\ \hline \boxed{} \end{array}$
$\begin{array}{r} 14 \\ -8 \\ \hline \boxed{} \end{array}$
$\begin{array}{r} 7 \\ +7 \\ \hline \boxed{} \end{array}$
$\begin{array}{r} 15 \\ -7 \\ \hline \boxed{} \end{array}$

3.
$\begin{array}{r} \boxed{} \\ +5 \\ \hline 13 \end{array}$
$\begin{array}{r} 16 \\ -\boxed{} \\ \hline 8 \end{array}$
$\begin{array}{r} 6 \\ +7 \\ \hline \boxed{} \end{array}$
$\begin{array}{r} 17 \\ -\boxed{} \\ \hline 8 \end{array}$
$\begin{array}{r} \boxed{} \\ +9 \\ \hline 14 \end{array}$
$\begin{array}{r} 14 \\ -\boxed{} \\ \hline 9 \end{array}$

4.
$\begin{array}{r} 7 \\ +\boxed{} \\ \hline 10 \end{array}$
$\begin{array}{r} 11 \\ -\boxed{} \\ \hline 5 \end{array}$
$\begin{array}{r} \boxed{} \\ +8 \\ \hline 13 \end{array}$
$\begin{array}{r} 18 \\ -9 \\ \hline \boxed{} \end{array}$
$\begin{array}{r} \boxed{} \\ +4 \\ \hline 11 \end{array}$
$\begin{array}{r} 15 \\ -\boxed{} \\ \hline 8 \end{array}$

5.
$\begin{array}{r} \boxed{} \\ +4 \\ \hline 12 \end{array}$
$\begin{array}{r} 10 \\ -\boxed{} \\ \hline 4 \end{array}$
$\begin{array}{r} 6 \\ +6 \\ \hline \boxed{} \end{array}$
$\begin{array}{r} 16 \\ -\boxed{} \\ \hline 7 \end{array}$
$\begin{array}{r} 8 \\ +\boxed{} \\ \hline 17 \end{array}$
$\begin{array}{r} 16 \\ -9 \\ \hline \boxed{} \end{array}$

Solve.

6. Jeff has 9 stamps. He gets 3 more. How many stamps does he have now?

_____ stamps

7. Gina has 15 postcards. 7 are from the United States. How many are not from the United States?

_____ postcards

Name _____

Reteach

Fact Families

Some fact families have two addition facts and two subtraction facts.

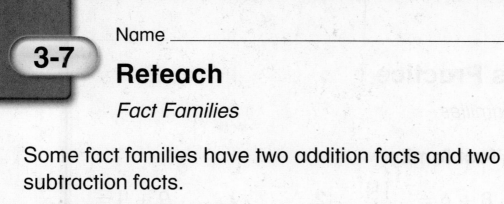

$9 + 7 = \underline{16}$ $16 - 7 = \underline{9}$

$7 + 9 = \underline{16}$ $16 - 9 = \underline{7}$

Some fact families have one addition fact and one subtraction fact.

$8 + 8 = \underline{16}$ $16 - 8 = \underline{8}$

Complete each fact family.

1. $9 + 4 = \underline{13}$ $13 - 9 = \underline{4}$

   $4 + 9 = \underline{13}$ $13 - 4 = \underline{9}$

2. $6 + 5 = \underline{}$ $11 - 5 = \underline{}$

   $5 + 6 = \underline{}$ $11 - 6 = \underline{}$

3. $9 + 8 = \underline{}$ $17 - 9 = \underline{}$

   $8 + 9 = \underline{}$ $17 - 8 = \underline{}$

4. $7 + 7 = \underline{}$ $14 - 7 = \underline{}$

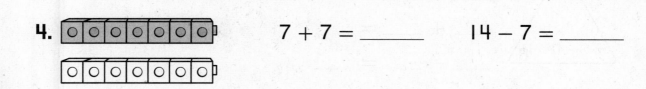

Name _____

Skills Practice

Fact Families

Complete each fact family.

1.

△ 14 / 8 / 6

$8 + 6 =$ __14__

$6 + 8 =$ _____

$14 - 8 =$ _____

$14 - 6 =$ _____

2.

△ 13 / 9 / 4

$9 + 4 =$ _____

$4 + 9 =$ _____

$13 - 9 =$ _____

$13 - 4 =$ _____

3.

△ 17 / 9 / 8

$8 + 9 =$ _____

$9 + 8 =$ _____

$17 - 8 =$ _____

$17 - 9 =$ _____

4.

△ 13 / 8 / 5

$5 + 8 =$ _____

$8 + 5 =$ _____

$13 - 5 =$ _____

$13 - 8 =$ _____

5.

△ 14 / 7 / 7

_____ $+ 7 = 14$

$14 - 7 =$ _____

6.

△ 18 / 9 / 9

_____ $+ 9 = 18$

$18 -$ _____ $= 9$

Solve. Write the number sentences in the fact family.

7. Lucas has 7 toy cars and 8 toy trucks. He has 15 toys in all.
Write the number sentences in the fact family.

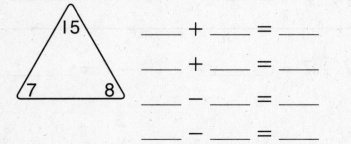

△ 15 / 7 / 8

_____ $+$ _____ $=$ _____

_____ $+$ _____ $=$ _____

_____ $-$ _____ $=$ _____

_____ $-$ _____ $=$ _____

3-8

Reteach (1)

Problem-Solving Investigation: Choose a Strategy

Kim's mom makes 13 blueberry pancakes. Kim eats some. There are 9 pancakes left when she finishes. How many pancakes did Kim eat?

Choose a problem-solving strategy to solve.

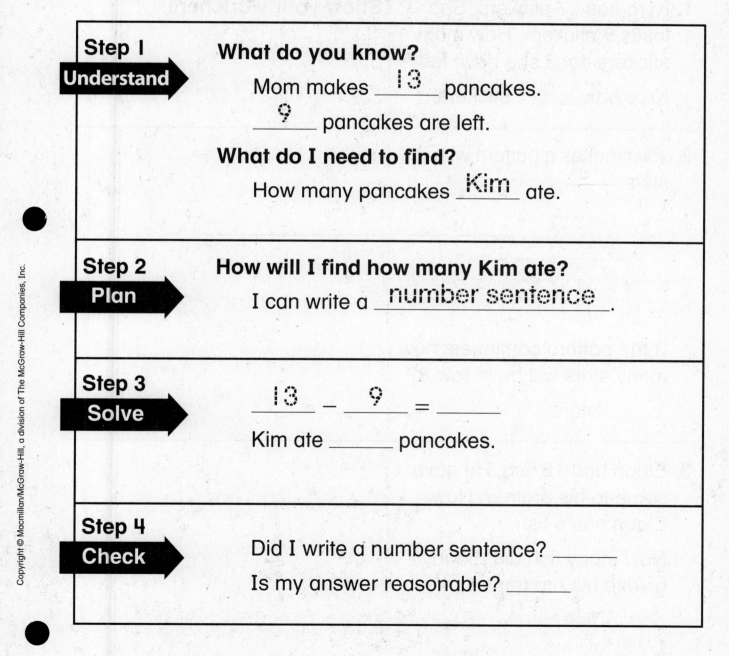

Step 1
Understand

What do you know?

Mom makes ___13___ pancakes.

___9___ pancakes are left.

What do I need to find?

How many pancakes ___Kim___ ate.

Step 2
Plan

How will I find how many Kim ate?

I can write a ___number sentence___.

Step 3
Solve

___13___ – ___9___ = _____

Kim ate _____ pancakes.

Step 4
Check

Did I write a number sentence? _____

Is my answer reasonable? _____

Name _____

Reteach (2)

Problem-Solving Investigation: Choose a Strategy

Choose a strategy and solve.

Problem-Solving Strategies
Find a pattern
Guess and check
Write a number sentence

1. Kyra has 17 stickers. She loses 9 stickers. How many stickers does she have left?

Krya has _____ stickers.

Show your work here.

2. Julia makes a pattern with stars.

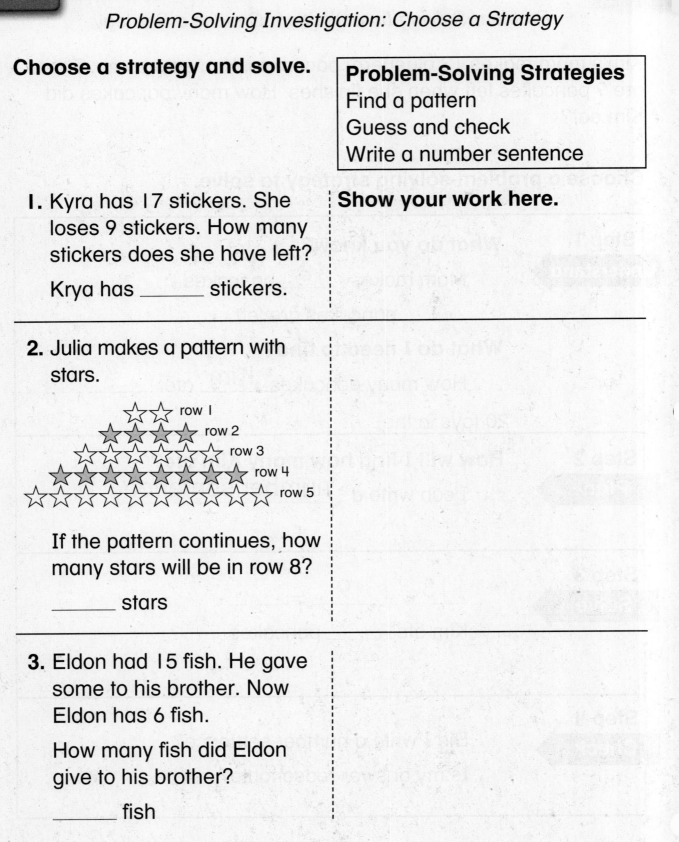

row 1
row 2
row 3
row 4
row 5

If the pattern continues, how many stars will be in row 8?

_____ stars

3. Eldon had 15 fish. He gave some to his brother. Now Eldon has 6 fish.

How many fish did Eldon give to his brother?

_____ fish

62

Name _____

Skills Practice

Problem-Solving Investigation: Choose a Strategy

Choose a strategy and solve.

Problem-Solving Strategies
Find a pattern
Guess and check
Write a number sentence

1. At the toy store there are 3 toys on the top shelf. 6 toys are on shelf two. 9 toys are on shelf 3. If the pattern continues, how many toys will be on shelf 6?

_____ toys

Show your work here.

2. There are 20 toys in the store window. 5 toys are trains. 4 toys are dolls. 6 toys are airplanes. The rest of the toys are games. How many toys are games?

_____ games

3. Three children are in line to pay for toys. Anna is not second. Ben is in line after Juan. Juan is not first. In what order will the children pay for their toys?

_____; _____; _____

Name _____

Reteach

Take a Survey

Use the survey to answer each question.

Look at your classmates. Make one tally mark to show what each classmate is wearing. Complete the chart.

Clothes in the Classroom	
Jeans	III
Sweaters	IIII
T-Shirts	II
Skirts	I

1. How many students are wearing sweaters?

_____5_____

2. How many students are wearing T-shirts?

_____2_____

3. Which got **more** marks, jeans or skirts?

_____Jeans_____

4. What item is worn the **least**?

_____Skirts_____

5. What item is worn the **most**?

_____Sweaters_____

Name _____

Skills Practice

Take a Survey

Use the survey to answer each question.

Ask classmates which hobby they like best. Use tally marks to record the data. Complete the chart.

Favorite Hobby	
Sports	⊞
Building Models	||
Painting	||||
Playing Music	⊞ ||| / = 3

Cookin

1. How many tally marks did playing music get?

_____ 6 _____

2. Which hobby has the most tally marks?

_____ playing music _____

3. Wes is starting a Craft Club. He wants to invite the students who like building models or painting. Write a number sentence to show how many students Wes should invite.

4 + 2 = 6

4. Sue wants to add cooking to the chart. Three students decide to change their vote from playing music to cooking. How many tallies are left for playing music?

_____ 3 _____

Name _____

Reteach

Picture Graphs

The picture graph shows the votes for favorite sport.

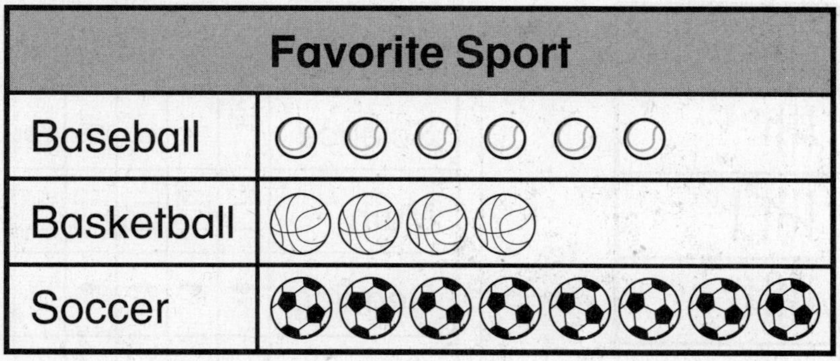

Favorite Sport	
Baseball	◯ ◯ ◯ ◯ ◯ ◯
Basketball	🏀 🏀 🏀 🏀
Soccer	⚽ ⚽ ⚽ ⚽ ⚽ ⚽ ⚽ ⚽

Use the tally chart to make a picture graph.

Favorite Vehicle	
Vehicle	**tally**
Car	||
Motorcycle	|||
Truck	卌

Favorite Vehicle	
Car	
Motorcycle	
Truck	

Key: Each vehicle stands for 1 vote.

1. How many more students voted for Truck than for Car?

   _____1_____ more students

2. Which vehicle is the favorite? ___trucks___

3. How many students voted in all? ___10___ students

Name _____

Skills Practice

Picture Graphs

**Some students voted for their favorite subject.
Use the tally chart to make a picture graph.**

Favorite Subject	
Science	⫻⫻
Math	⫻⫻ I
Reading	IIII
Art	⫻⫻

Favorite Subject

Science	🔬	🔬	🔬	🔬	🔬		
Math	📄	📄	📄	📄	📄	📄	
Reading	📖	📖	📖	📖			
Art	🎨	🎨	🎨	🎨	🎨		

Key: Each symbol stands for 1 vote.

Use the graph to answer each question.

1. How many students voted for Reading?

   ____4____ students

2. How many more students voted for Math than voted
   for Art? ____1____ student

3. How many students in all voted for Science and Art? __10__
   students

4. Lila wants to vote for the subject with the least votes. Which

   subject should she vote for? __Reading__

5. Rick, Tom, and Cindy like Science the best. If their votes
   are added to the survey, will Science have the

   most votes? __yes__

Name _____

Reteach

Analyze Picture Graphs

Use the picture graph to answer the questions.

Favorite Sports									
Basketball	🏀	🏀	🏀	🏀	🏀	🏀			
Baseball	⚾	⚾	⚾						
Soccer	⚽	⚽	⚽	⚽					

Key: Each symbol = 2 votes

I. How many people voted for their favorite sport?

_____ people

2. According to the graph, what is the most popular sport?

_____

3. How many people voted for soccer?

_____ people

4. Did more people choose basketball or the other sports combined?

_____

5. How would the graph change if the people surveyed had another sport to pick from?

_____

_____

Name _____

Skills Practice

Analyze Picture Graphs

Use the picture graph to answer the questions.

Winter Snow									
November	🎃								
December	❄	❄	❄						
January	✋	✋	✋	✋	✋				
February	🌷	🌷	🌷	🌷					
March	☀	☀							

Key: Each symbol = 1 inch of snow

1. What month got the least amount of snow?

_____

2. Which month had more snow, December or February?

_____

3. How many inches of snow fell in January? _____

4. Why do you think the chart stopped at March?

_____

_____

5. Can you think of another way you could record the weather using a picture graph?

_____

Name _____

Reteach (1)

Problem-Solving Strategy: Make a Table

Gloria buys seeds for her garden.
Each packet of seeds has 7 seeds inside.
Gloria buys 3 packets.
How many seeds does she buy altogether?

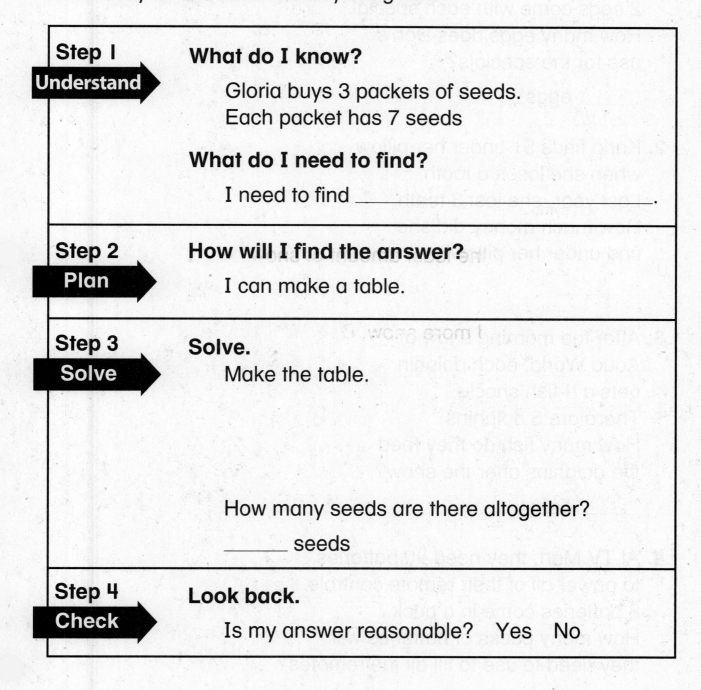

Step 1
Understand

What do I know?

Gloria buys 3 packets of seeds.
Each packet has 7 seeds

What do I need to find?

I need to find _____.

Step 2
Plan

How will I find the answer?

I can make a table.

Step 3
Solve

Solve.
Make the table.

How many seeds are there altogether?

_____ seeds

Step 4
Check

Look back.

Is my answer reasonable?   Yes   No

Name _____

Reteach (2)

Problem-Solving Strategy: Make a Table

Make a table to solve.

1. Don's Breakfast Diner sells
   6 morning specials.
   2 eggs come with each special.
   How many eggs does Don's
   use for the specials?

   _____ eggs

   Show your work here.

2. Karla finds $1 under her pillow
   when she loses a tooth.
   Last year, she lost 3 teeth.
   How much money did she
   find under her pillow?

   _____

3. After the morning show at
   Aqua World, each dolphin
   gets a 4-fish snack.
   There are 5 dolphins.
   How many fish do they feed
   the dolphins after the show?

   _____ fish

4. At TV Mart, they need 40 batteries
   to power all of their remote controls.
   8 batteries come in a pack.
   How many packs of batteries will
   they need to use to fill all the remotes?

   _____ packs

Name _____

Skills Practice

Problem-Solving Strategy: Make a Table

Make a table to solve.

1. The school cafeteria is 60 eggs short for breakfast! Eggs are sold in cartons of 12. How many cartons do they need to buy to have enough eggs?

_____ cartons

Show your work here.

2. 7 baseball cards come in a pack. Justin buys 4 packs. How many cards does he get?

_____ cards

3. In Marisol's high school English class, each student gets 3 different books. There are 25 students in her class. How many books do they pass out altogether?

_____ books

4. Sung's favorite snack comes in packages of 5. If he has 1 snack a day, how many packages will Sung need for the next 15 days?

_____ packages

Name _____

Reteach

Bar Graphs

Bar graphs use bars to show data. You can make a bar graph with data you read. Read the data to complete the bar graph.

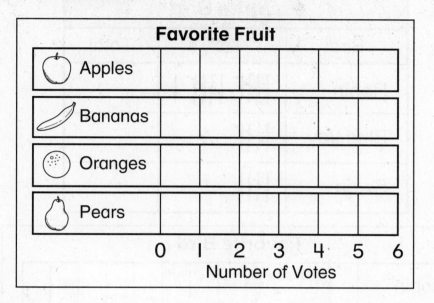

Favorite Fruit

Data:

Four people voted for apples. Show this on the graph.

Five people voted for oranges. Show this on the graph.

Two people voted for pears. Show this on the graph.

Three people voted for bananas. Show this on the graph.

Answer each question.

1. What is the title of this bar graph? _____

2. How many kinds of fruit are shown in the graph? _____ kinds

3. How many votes did apples get? _____ votes

4. What is the favorite fruit? _____

Name _____

Skills Practice

Bar Graphs

Use the tally chart to make a bar graph. Color one box for each vote. Then answer each question.

Favorite Bird		
Bird	Tally	Total
Robin	~~HHT~~ ~~HHT~~ I	11
Blue Jay	~~HHT~~	5
Swan	IIII	4

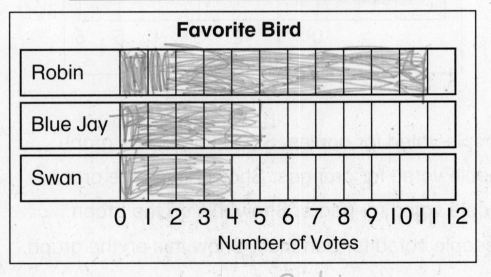

Favorite Bird

Robin

Blue Jay

Swan

0 1 2 3 4 5 6 7 8 9 10 11 12
Number of Votes

1. Which bird got the most votes? ___Robin___

2. How many more students voted for the *robin* than the *swan*?
   ___7___ students

3. Blue jays received ___5___ votes.

4. How many students voted in all? ___20___ students

Name _____

Reteach

Analyze Bar Graphs

Use the bar graph to complete the sentences.

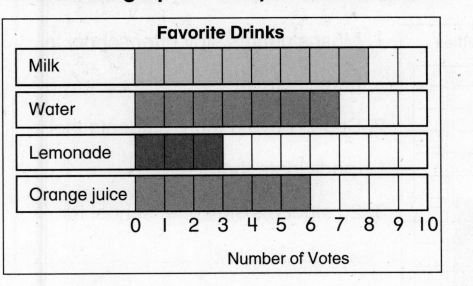

1. Students' favorite drink is _____.

2. Milk has 5 more votes than _____.

3. 13 students voted for _____ or _____.

4. How many people were surveyed? _____ people.

5. How might this graph help the people who run the cafeteria?

_____

_____

6. If the cafeteria could only serve two drinks, which two should they serve?

_____

Why? _____

_____

Name _____

Skills Practice

Analyze Bar Graphs

Use the bar graph to complete the sentences.

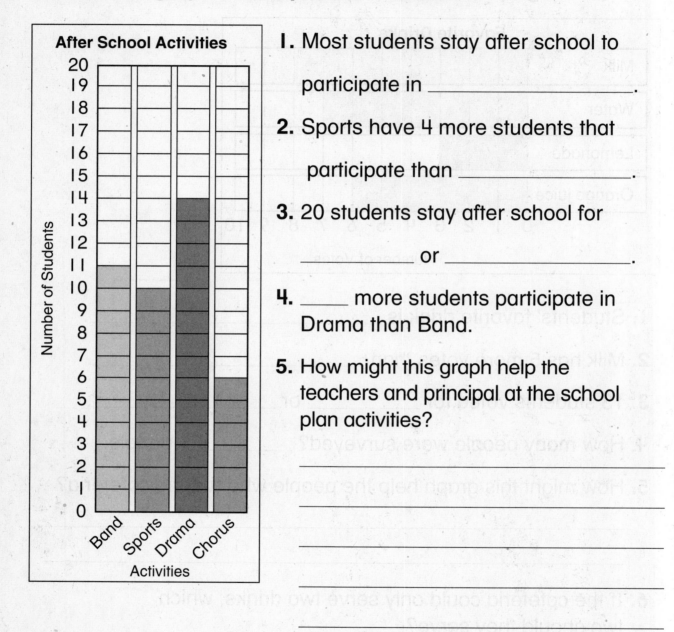

After School Activities

Number of Students

20 19 18 17 16 15 14 13 12 11 10 9 8 7 6 5 4 3 2 1 0

Band   Sports   Drama   Chorus

Activities

1. Most students stay after school to participate in _____.

2. Sports have 4 more students that participate than _____.

3. 20 students stay after school for _____ or _____.

4. _____ more students participate in Drama than Band.

5. How might this graph help the teachers and principal at the school plan activities?

_____

_____

_____

_____

_____

Reteach

Describe Events

**Tell if the event is *more likely* or *less likely*
to happen.**

1. 2 red ▨ and 5 green ▨ are in a bag. You are _____ to pick a
   red ▨ than a green ▨. Circle.

   more likely   less likely

2. Now place 2 red ▨ and 5 green ▨ in a bag or a bucket. Draw
   ten times without looking. Record your results in the tally chart.

Color Chosen	
Color	Tally
Red	
Green	

3. 6 orange ▨ and 3 purple ▨ are in a bag. You are _____ to pick
   an orange ▨ than a purple ▨. Circle.

   more likely   less likely

4. Now place 6 orange ▨ and 3 purple ▨ in a bag or a bucket. Draw
   ten times without looking. Record your results in the tally chart.

Color Chosen	
Color	Tally
Orange	
Purple	

Name _____

Skills Practice

Describe Events

Tell if the event is *more likely* or *less likely* to happen.

1. 6 green ▣ and 4 red ▢ are in a bag. You are _____ to pick a green ▢ than a red ▣. Circle.

   more likely   less likely

2. Place 6 green ▣ and 4 red ▢ in a bag or a bucket. Draw ten times without looking. Record your results in the chart.

Color Chosen	
Color	Tally
Green	
Red	

3. Justin has 8 black socks in his drawer and 12 white socks. If he pulls one sock out of the drawer without looking, is he *more likely* or *less likely* to pull out a white sock? _____

   Explain. _____

4. Andrea has a bag of marbles. All her marbles are 2 colors: silver and gold. She has 10 gold marbles in the bag and 5 silver. Is she *more likely* or *less likely* to pull out a silver marble? _____

   Explain. _____

Name _____

Reteach (1)

Problem-Solving Investigation: Choose a Strategy

Aaron has 3 muffin pans. Each pan can hold 6 muffins. How many muffins can Aaron bake?

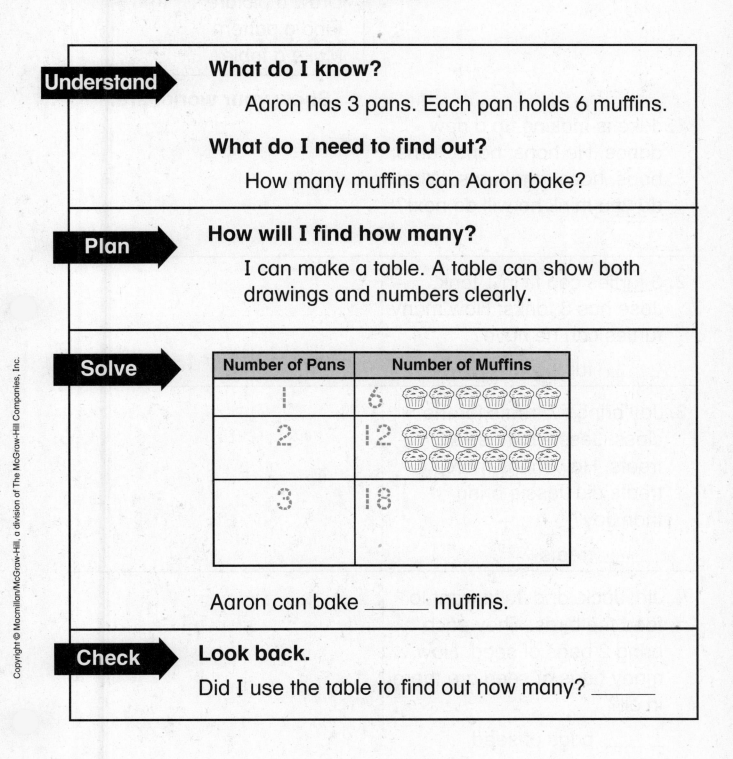

Understand ▶

What do I know?

Aaron has 3 pans. Each pan holds 6 muffins.

What do I need to find out?

How many muffins can Aaron bake?

Plan ▶

How will I find how many?

I can make a table. A table can show both drawings and numbers clearly.

Solve ▶

Number of Pans	Number of Muffins
1	6
2	12
3	18

Aaron can bake _____ muffins.

Check ▶

Look back.

Did I use the table to find out how many? _____

Name _____

Reteach (2)

Problem-Solving Investigation: Choose a Strategy

Choose a strategy. Solve.

Problem-Solving Strategies
Draw a picture
Find a pattern
Make a table

Show your work here.

1. Jake is making up a new dance. He hops, hops, turns, hops, hops, and turns. What do you think he will do next?

_____

2. 3 turtles can fit in 1 tank. Jose has 3 tanks. How many turtles can he have?

_____ turtles

3. Joy brings 7 treats for the class. Jessie brings 14 treats. How many more treats did Jessie bring than Joy?

_____ treats

4. Jin, Jack, and Julia want to feed the birds. They each bring 2 bags of seed. How many bags of seed are there in all?

_____ bags of seed

Name _____

Skills Practice

Problem-Solving Investigation: Choose a Strategy

Choose a strategy. Solve.

Problem-Solving Strategies
  Draw a picture
  Find a pattern
  Make a table

Show your work here.

I. Shandra is giving a treat bag to each of her 3 friends. She puts 4 pear slices in each bag. How many pear slices are there in all?

_____ pear slices

2. Liam is writing the number of eggs his hens have. I hen has 2 eggs. 2 hens have 4 eggs. 3 hens have 6 eggs. Liam guesses that 4 hens will have 8 eggs. Is this a good guess?

_____

3. Kiki, Greg, and Seth are making snowmen. Each snowman needs I carrot for a nose. Kiki brings 4 carrots. Greg brings 2. Seth brings 5. Are there enough carrots to make 12 snowmen?_____ How many can they make?

_____ snowmen

5-1

Reteach

Add Tens

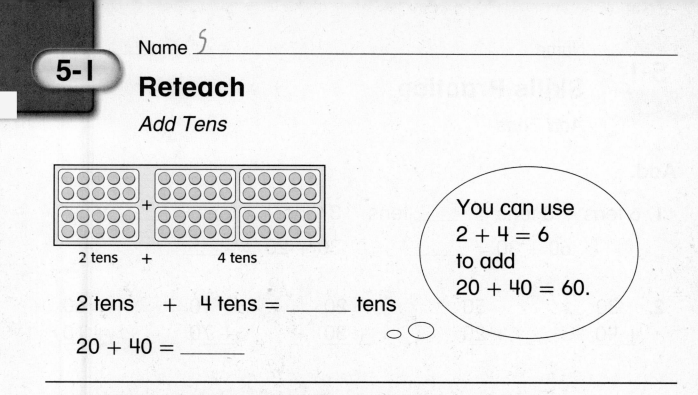

2 tens   +   4 tens

You can use
2 + 4 = 6
to add
20 + 40 = 60.

2 tens   +   4 tens = _____ tens

20 + 40 = _____

Add. Use the addition facts and counters to help.

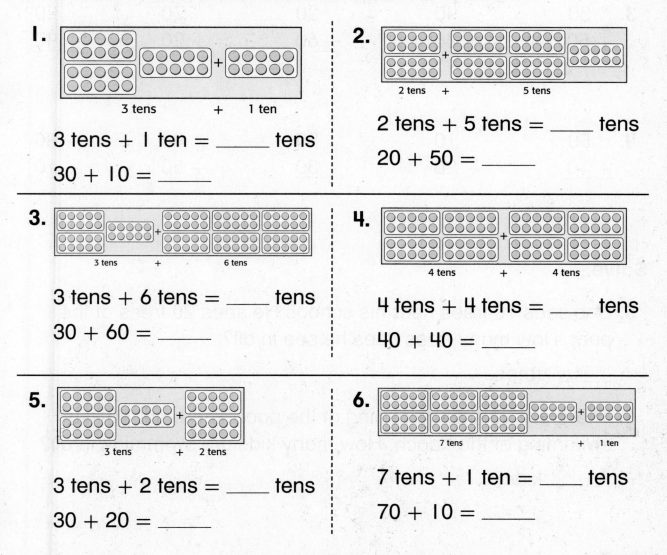

1.

3 tens   +   1 ten

3 tens + 1 ten = _____ tens

30 + 10 = _____

2.

2 tens   +   5 tens

2 tens + 5 tens = _____ tens

20 + 50 = _____

3.

3 tens   +   6 tens

3 tens + 6 tens = _____ tens

30 + 60 = _____

4.

4 tens   +   4 tens

4 tens + 4 tens = _____ tens

40 + 40 = _____

5.

3 tens   +   2 tens

3 tens + 2 tens = _____ tens

30 + 20 = _____

6.

7 tens   +   1 ten

7 tens + 1 ten = _____ tens

70 + 10 = _____

Name _____

Skills Practice

Add Tens

Add.

1. 6 tens + 3 tens = _____ tens   3 tens + 2 tens = _____ tens

   60 + 30 = _____   30 + 20 = _____

2.
30	50	20	10	60
+ 40	+ 20	+ 30	+ 70	+ 10

3.
30	40	20	70	40
+ 50	+ 20	+ 60	+ 20	+ 40

4.
50	10	30	40	80
+ 10	+ 20	+ 30	+ 50	+ 10

Solve.

5. Bob sees 10 trees near his school. He sees 20 trees at the park. How many trees does he see in all?

   _____ trees

6. There are 30 kids swimming at the pool. There are 40 kids swimming at the beach. How many kids are swimming in all?

   _____ kids

Name _____

Reteach

Count On Tens and Ones

Count on to add. Use the hundred chart to help.

1	2	3	4	5	6	7	8	9	10
11	12	13	14	15	16	17	18	19	20
21	22	23	24	25	26	27	28	29	30
31	32	33	34	35	36	37	38	39	40
41	42	43	44	45	46	47	48	49	50
51	52	53	54	55	56	57	58	59	60
61	62	63	64	65	66	67	68	69	70
71	72	73	74	75	76	77	78	79	80
81	82	83	84	85	86	87	88	89	90
91	92	93	94	95	96	97	98	99	100

$45 + 20 =$ _____

Count on by tens to add.

45, _____, _____

$21 + 3 =$ _____

Count on by ones to add.

21, _____, _____, _____

Count on to add. Write the sum.

1. $18 + 30 =$ _____ Count by tens. 18, _____, _____, _____

2. $31 + 4 =$ _____ Count by ones. 31, ____, ____, ____, ____

3. $65 + 3 =$ _____

4. $37 + 20 =$ _____

5. $57 + 10 =$ _____

6. $41 + 40 =$ _____

7. $21 + 8 =$ _____

8. $36 + 3 =$ _____

9. $43 + 50 =$ _____

10. $62 + 7 =$ _____

Name _Skylar_

Skills Practice

Count On Tens and Ones

Count on to add. Write the sum.

1. $43 + 20 =$ _____

$35 + 30 =$ _____

2. $18 + 40 =$ _____

$51 + 10 =$ _____

3.
$$\begin{array}{r} 62 \\ + 10 \\ \hline \end{array}$$
$$\begin{array}{r} 24 \\ + 30 \\ \hline \end{array}$$
$$\begin{array}{r} 40 \\ + 28 \\ \hline \end{array}$$
$$\begin{array}{r} 13 \\ + 70 \\ \hline \end{array}$$
$$\begin{array}{r} 55 \\ + 20 \\ \hline \end{array}$$

4.
$$\begin{array}{r} 20 \\ + 49 \\ \hline \end{array}$$
$$\begin{array}{r} 34 \\ + 20 \\ \hline \end{array}$$
$$\begin{array}{r} 5 \\ + 44 \\ \hline \end{array}$$
$$\begin{array}{r} 80 \\ + 11 \\ \hline \end{array}$$
$$\begin{array}{r} 48 \\ + 40 \\ \hline \end{array}$$

5.
$$\begin{array}{r} 35 \\ + 10 \\ \hline \end{array}$$
$$\begin{array}{r} 20 \\ + 53 \\ \hline \end{array}$$
$$\begin{array}{r} 30 \\ + 13 \\ \hline \end{array}$$
$$\begin{array}{r} 36 \\ + 50 \\ \hline \end{array}$$
$$\begin{array}{r} 17 \\ + 30 \\ \hline \end{array}$$

6.
$$\begin{array}{r} 44 \\ + 40 \\ \hline \end{array}$$
$$\begin{array}{r} 38 \\ + 20 \\ \hline \end{array}$$
$$\begin{array}{r} 60 \\ + 18 \\ \hline \end{array}$$
$$\begin{array}{r} 70 \\ + 23 \\ \hline \end{array}$$
$$\begin{array}{r} 57 \\ + 10 \\ \hline \end{array}$$

Solve.

7. There are 30 children in the second grade. There are 45 children in the third grade. How many children are there in all?

_____ children

8. The school gets 40 new math books. They also get 32 new spelling books. How many new books do they have now?

_____ books

Name _____

Reteach (1)

Problem-Solving Strategy: Work Backward

Mike scores 10 more points than Sara.
Sara scores 5 more points than Des does.
Des scores 6 points.
How many points does Mike score?

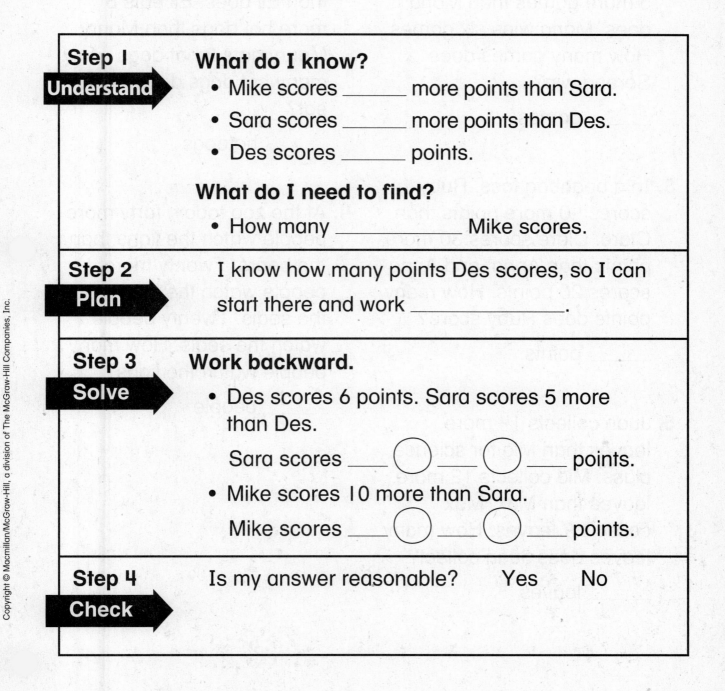

Step 1
Understand

What do I know?

• Mike scores _____ more points than Sara.

• Sara scores _____ more points than Des.

• Des scores _____ points.

What do I need to find?

• How many _____ Mike scores.

Step 2
Plan

I know how many points Des scores, so I can start there and work _____.

Step 3
Solve

Work backward.

• Des scores 6 points. Sara scores 5 more than Des.

Sara scores ____ ◯ ____ ◯ ____ points.

• Mike scores 10 more than Sara.

Mike scores ____ ◯ ____ ◯ ____ points.

Step 4
Check

Is my answer reasonable?   Yes   No

5-3

Reteach (2)

Problem-Solving Strategy: Work Backward

Work backward to solve.

1. Serena wins 7 more games than Lex does. Lex wins 5 more games than Maria does. Maria wins six games. How many games does Serena win?

   _____ games

2. In a hot dog-eating contest, Yoshi eats 10 more hot dogs than Eli does. Eli eats 6 more hot dogs than Maury. Maury eats 8 hot dogs. How many hot dogs does Yoshi eat?

   _____ hotdogs

3. In a beanbag toss, Ruby scores 40 more points than Clare. Clare scores 30 more points than Anna, and Anna scores 20 points. How many points does Ruby score?

   _____ points

4. At the zoo today, forty more people watch the lions than the bears. Twenty more people watch the bears than the seals. Twenty people watch the seals. How many people watch the lions?

   _____ people

5. Juan collects 14 more leaves than Mia for science class. Mia collects 12 more leaves than Max. Max collects 9 leaves. How many leaves does Juan collect?

   _____ leaves

5-3

Skills Practice

Problem-Solving Strategy: Work Backward

Solve. Work backward. Show your work.

1. Ann's dog does 4 more tricks than Ben's dog. Ben's dog does 9 more tricks than Lisa's dog. Lisa's dog does 5 tricks. How many tricks does Ann's dog do?

_____

_____ tricks

2. Green Stable has 12 more horses than Happy Glen. Happy Glen has 9 more horses than Sun Farm. Sun Farm has 7 horses. How many horses does Green Stable have?

_____

_____ horses

3. Dan has twenty fish in 5 different tanks. Ahmal has 8 more fish than Dan. Their friend Andi has 10 more fish than Ahmal. How many fish does Andi have?

_____

_____ fish

4. In one week, Kitty Rescue saves 12 cats. That same week, Caring Paws saves 6 more cats than Kitty Rescue. Here Kitty Kitty saves 10 more cats than Caring Paws. How many cats did Here Kitty Kitty save?

_____

_____ cats

5. Dora's Diner has 3 more breakfast specials than the Tip-Top Grill. The Tip-Top Grill has 11 more breakfast specials than Charlie's Cafe. Charlie's Cafe has 6 breakfast specials. How many breakfast specials does Dora's Diner have?

_____

_____ specials

43 + 8 =

Name _Skyler_

Reteach

Regroup Ones as Tens

Add. Regroup when you have 10 ones.

Step 1

$$18$$
$$+ \ 6$$

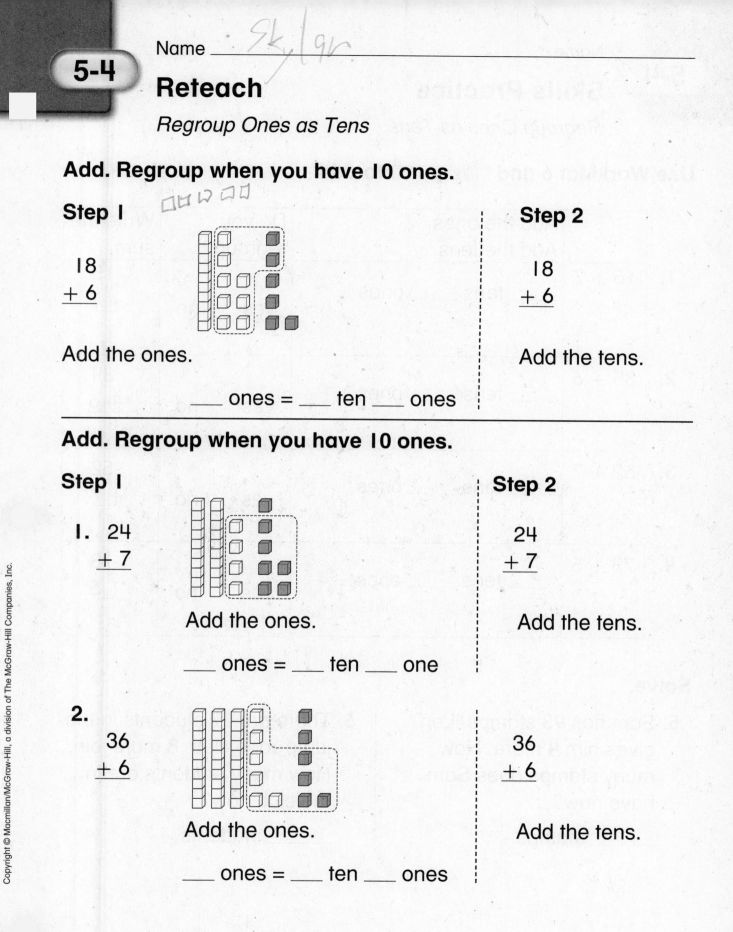

Add the ones.

___ ones = ___ ten ___ ones

Step 2

$$18$$
$$+ \ 6$$

Add the tens.

Add. Regroup when you have 10 ones.

Step 1

1. $$24$$
    $$+ \ 7$$

Add the ones.

___ ones = ___ ten ___ one

Step 2

$$24$$
$$+ \ 7$$

Add the tens.

2.

$$36$$
$$+ \ 6$$

Add the ones.

___ ones = ___ ten ___ ones

$$36$$
$$+ \ 6$$

Add the tens.

Name _____

Skills Practice

Regroup Ones as Tens

Use WorkMat 6 and ⬚⬚⬚⬚⬚⬚ **to add.**

		Add the ones. Add the tens.	Do you regroup?	Write the sum.
1.	15 + 7	_____ tens _____ ones	yes no	15 + 7
2.	34 + 6	_____ tens _____ ones	yes no	34 + 6
3.	52 + 7	_____ tens _____ ones	yes no	52 + 7
4.	73 + 5	_____ tens _____ ones	yes no	73 + 5

Solve.

5. Sam has 93 stamps. Len gives him 4 more. How many stamps does Sam have now?

_____ stamps

6. There are 17 students in the jump-rope club. 8 more join. How many students are in the club now?

_____ students

Name _____

Reteach

Add One-Digit Numbers and Two-Digit Numbers

Find the sum. Regroup if you need to.

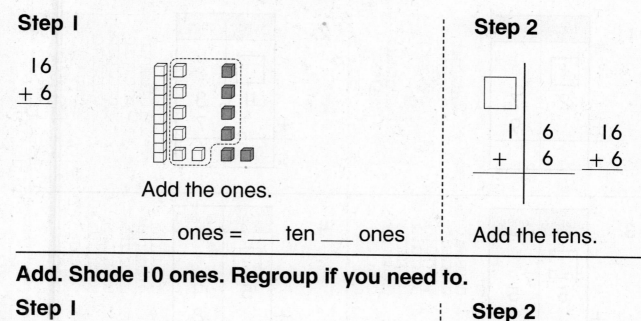

Step 1

16
+ 6

Add the ones.

___ ones = ___ ten ___ ones

Step 2

1 6   16
+ 6   + 6

Add the tens.

Add. Shade 10 ones. Regroup if you need to.

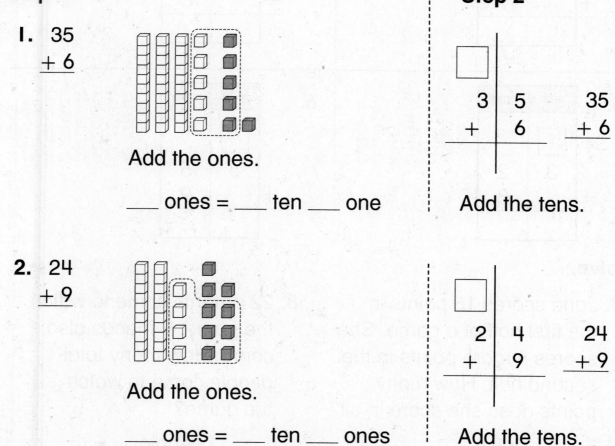

Step 1

1. 35
   + 6

Add the ones.

___ ones = ___ ten ___ one

Step 2

3 5   35
+ 6   + 6

Add the tens.

2. 24
   + 9

Add the ones.

___ ones = ___ ten ___ ones

2 4   24
+ 9   + 9

Add the tens.

Name _____

Skills Practice

Add One-Digit Numbers and Two-Digit Numbers

Use WorkMat 6 and ▱▱▱▱▱ **to add.**

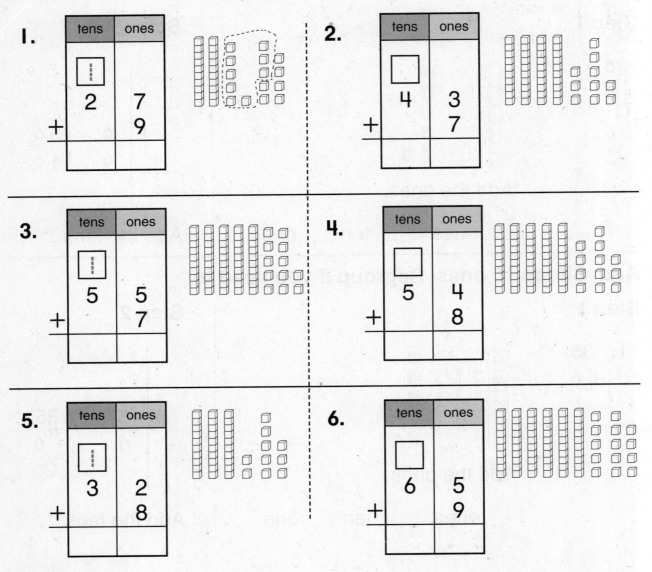

1.

tens	ones
2	7
+	9

2.

tens	ones
4	3
+	7

3.

tens	ones
5	5
+	7

4.

tens	ones
5	4
+	8

5.

tens	ones
3	2
+	8

6.

tens	ones
6	5
+	9

Solve.

7. Jana scores 18 points in the first half of a game. She scores 6 more points in the second half. How many points does she score in all?

_____ points

8. 22 parents come to watch the game. 9 friends also come. How many total people come to watch the game?

_____ people

Name _____

Reteach

Add Two-Digit Numbers

June has 28 stickers.
Pam gives her 16 more stickers.
How many stickers does June have now?

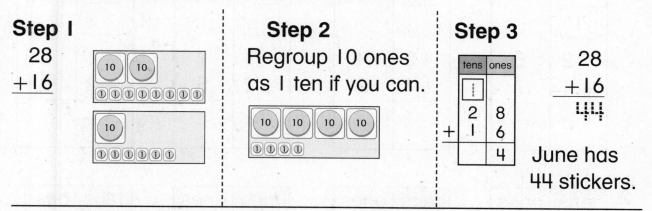

Step 1

28
+16

Step 2

Regroup 10 ones
as 1 ten if you can.

Step 3

tens	ones
2	8
+ 1	6
	4

28
+16
44

June has
44 stickers.

Add. You can use counters to help. Regroup if you need to.

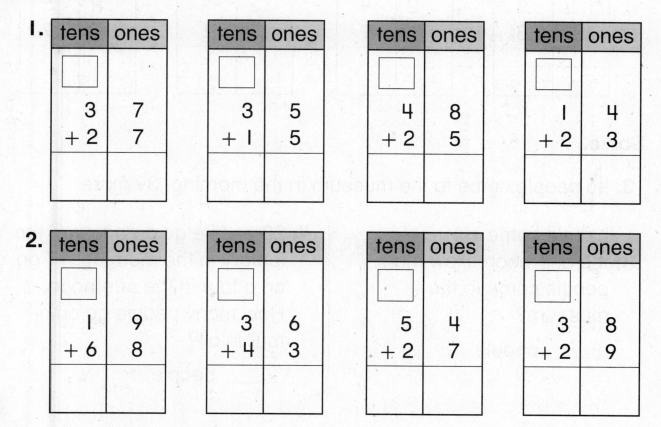

1.

tens	ones
3	7
+ 2	7

tens	ones
3	5
+ 1	5

tens	ones
4	8
+ 2	5

tens	ones
1	4
+ 2	3

2.

tens	ones
1	9
+ 6	8

tens	ones
3	6
+ 4	3

tens	ones
5	4
+ 2	7

tens	ones
3	8
+ 2	9

Name _____

Skills Practice

Add Two-Digit Numbers

Use WorkMat 6 and ⬚⬚⬚⬚⬚⬚⬚⬚ **to add.**

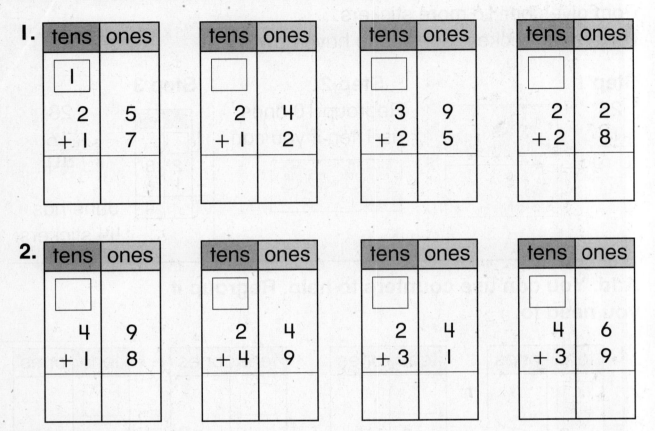

1.

tens	ones
☐ 1	
2	5
+ 1	7

tens	ones
☐	
2	4
+ 1	2

tens	ones
☐	
3	9
+ 2	5

tens	ones
☐	
2	2
+ 2	8

2.

tens	ones
☐	
4	9
+ 1	8

tens	ones
☐	
2	4
+ 4	9

tens	ones
☐	
2	4
+ 3	1

tens	ones
☐	
4	6
+ 3	9

Solve.

3. 46 people come to the museum in the morning. 39 more people come in the afternoon. How many people come to the museum?

_____ people

4. 20 people go on a tour of the factory in the morning. 17 go on a tour in the afternoon. How many people go on a tour in all?

_____ people

Reteach

Estimate Sums

An estimate is an answer that is close to
the exact answer.
If you do not need an exact answer, you
can estimate.

1	2	3	4	5	6	7	8	9	10
11	12	13	⑭	15	16	17	18	19	20
21	22	23	24	25	26	㉗	28	29	30
31	32	33	34	35	36	37	38	39	40
41	42	43	44	45	46	47	48	49	50
51	52	53	54	55	56	57	58	59	60
61	62	63	64	65	66	67	68	69	70
71	72	73	74	75	76	77	78	79	80
81	82	83	84	85	86	87	88	89	90
91	92	93	94	95	96	97	98	99	100

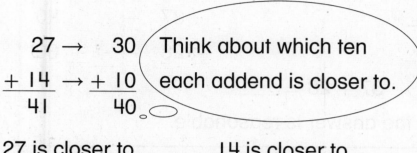

$$27 \rightarrow \quad 30$$
$$+\ 14 \rightarrow +\ 10$$
$$\overline{\quad 41 \qquad 40}$$

Think about which ten
each addend is closer to.

27 is closer to _____. 14 is closer to _____.

27 + 14 is about _____.

41 is close to 40, so the answer is reasonable.

Round each addend to the nearest ten.
Estimate the sum.

1.
$$\begin{array}{r} 45 \\ +14 \\ \hline 59 \end{array} \qquad +\underline{\quad\quad}$$

2.
$$\begin{array}{r} 82 \\ +12 \\ \hline 94 \end{array} \qquad +\underline{\quad\quad}$$

3.
$$\begin{array}{r} 76 \\ +12 \\ \hline 88 \end{array} \qquad +\underline{\quad\quad}$$

4.
$$\begin{array}{r} 31 \\ +28 \\ \hline 59 \end{array} \qquad +\underline{\quad\quad}$$

5.
$$\begin{array}{r} 38 \\ +28 \\ \hline 66 \end{array} \qquad +\underline{\quad\quad}$$

6.
$$\begin{array}{r} 16 \\ +49 \\ \hline 65 \end{array} \qquad +\underline{\quad\quad}$$

7.
$$\begin{array}{r} 47 \\ +29 \\ \hline 76 \end{array} \qquad +\underline{\quad\quad}$$

8.
$$\begin{array}{r} 12 \\ +59 \\ \hline 71 \end{array} \qquad +\underline{\quad\quad}$$

9.
$$\begin{array}{r} 83 \\ +16 \\ \hline 99 \end{array} \qquad +\underline{\quad\quad}$$

Name _____

Skills Practice

Estimate Sums

You can estimate when you don't need an exact answer, or to check addition. A number line can help you estimate.

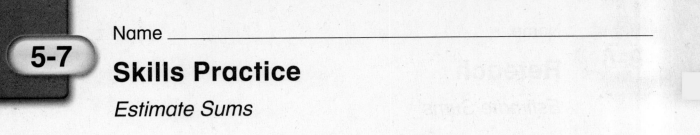

30 31 32 33 34 35 36 37 38 39 40 41 42 43 44 45 46 47 48 49 50

37 is closer to _____.   37 → 40

28 is closer to _____.   + 28 → + 30

40 + 30 is _____.   37 + 28 = ____

65 is close to 70, so the answer is reasonable.

**Add. Then round each addend to the nearest ten.
Estimate the sum.**

1. 28 → 30 + 28 → + 30	**2.** 38 → + 49 → +	**3.** 32 → + 41 → +
4. 48 + 33 + ___	**5.** 31 + 32 + ___	**6.** 22 + 48 + ___

Solve. Make an estimate.

7. Hugo has 43 cents. Olive has 48 cents. Together, do they have enough to buy a box of raisins that costs 85 cents? Prove your answer.

_____

8. Kendra has 27 cents. Mikey has 43 cents. Do they have enough money to buy a box of popcorn that costs 90 cents? Explain.

_____

Name _____

Reteach

Add Three Two-Digit Numbers

You can use addition strategies to help you add three addends.

Look for doubles.

Look for a ten.

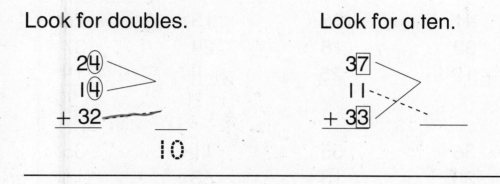

$$
\begin{array}{r}
2\textcircled{4} \\
1\textcircled{4} \\
+\ 32 \\
\hline
\end{array}
$$

10

$$
\begin{array}{r}
3\boxed{7} \\
11 \\
+\ 3\boxed{3} \\
\hline
\end{array}
$$

Add. Circle the doubles. Put a box on the tens.

1.
$$
\begin{array}{r}
1\textcircled{4} \\
2\textcircled{4} \\
+\ 13 \\
\hline
51
\end{array}
\qquad
\begin{array}{r}
42 \\
27 \\
+\ 12 \\
\hline
81
\end{array}
\qquad
\begin{array}{r}
27 \\
10 \\
+\ 13 \\
\hline
50
\end{array}
\qquad
\begin{array}{r}
29 \\
42 \\
+\ 21 \\
\hline
92
\end{array}
\qquad
\begin{array}{r}
24 \\
11 \\
+\ 26 \\
\hline
81
\end{array}
\qquad
\begin{array}{r}
48 \\
11 \\
+\ 12 \\
\hline
71
\end{array}
$$

2.
$$
\begin{array}{r}
17 \\
30 \\
+\ 13 \\
\hline
60
\end{array}
\qquad
\begin{array}{r}
23 \\
26 \\
+\ 46 \\
\hline
95
\end{array}
\qquad
\begin{array}{r}
45 \\
13 \\
+\ 15 \\
\hline
73
\end{array}
\qquad
\begin{array}{r}
6 \\
24 \\
+\ 40 \\
\hline
70
\end{array}
\qquad
\begin{array}{r}
10 \\
57 \\
+\ 23 \\
\hline
90
\end{array}
\qquad
\begin{array}{r}
23 \\
16 \\
+\ 33 \\
\hline
72
\end{array}
$$

3.
$$
\begin{array}{r}
32 \\
18 \\
+\ 11 \\
\hline
61
\end{array}
\qquad
\begin{array}{r}
13 \\
36 \\
+\ 46 \\
\hline
95
\end{array}
\qquad
\begin{array}{r}
55 \\
20 \\
+\ 15 \\
\hline
90
\end{array}
\qquad
\begin{array}{r}
19 \\
41 \\
+\ 13 \\
\hline
73
\end{array}
\qquad
\begin{array}{r}
37 \\
17 \\
+\ 32 \\
\hline
86
\end{array}
\qquad
\begin{array}{r}
21 \\
17 \\
+\ 13 \\
\hline
51
\end{array}
$$

Name _Skylar_

Skills Practice

Add Three Two-Digit Numbers

Look for two numbers in the ones column that make a ten or a double. Circle them. Add.

1.
23	41	35	13	26
14	32	18	24	37
+ 27	+ 12	+ 25	+ 4	+ 14
64	85	78	41	77

2.
8	36	55	11	35
20	28	13	63	16
+ 12	+ 32	+ 14	+ 24	+ 34
40	96	82	98	85

3.
14	52	44	19	24
13	20	16	68	3
+ 14	+ 11	+ 22	+ 12	+ 25
41	83	82	99	52

4.
21	37	14	62	43
18	12	45	11	15
+ 21	+ 27	+ 3	+ 23	+ 22
60	78	62	96	80

Solve.

5. There are 34 children in first grade. There are 27 in second grade. There are 31 in third grade. How many children are there in all?

____92____ children

6. 13 students play the bells. 16 students play the drums. 24 students play the recorder. How many total students play instruments?

____53____ students

5-9

Reteach (1)

Problem-Solving Investigation: Choose a Strategy

On a math test, Edie scores 10 points more than Jack. Jack's score is 5 points more than Dee's. Dee scores 73 points. How many points does Edie score?

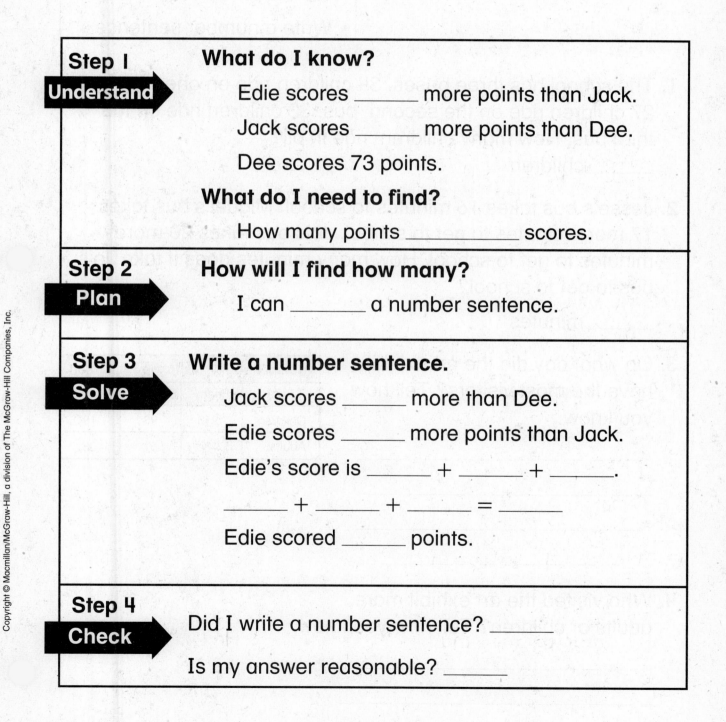

Step 1 **Understand**	**What do I know?** Edie scores _____ more points than Jack. Jack scores _____ more points than Dee. Dee scores 73 points. **What do I need to find?** How many points _____ scores.
Step 2 **Plan**	**How will I find how many?** I can _____ a number sentence.
Step 3 **Solve**	**Write a number sentence.** Jack scores _____ more than Dee. Edie scores _____ more points than Jack. Edie's score is _____ + _____ + _____. _____ + _____ + _____ = _____ Edie scored _____ points.
Step 4 **Check**	Did I write a number sentence? _____ Is my answer reasonable? _____

Name _____

Reteach (2)

Problem-Solving Investigation: Choose a Strategy

Choose a strategy. Solve.

Problem-Solving Strategies
• Draw a picture
• Work backward
• Write a number sentence

1. The school has three buses. 34 children ride on one bus. 27 children ride on the second bus. 33 children ride on the third bus. How many children ride in all?

   _____ children

2. Jesse's bus takes 16 minutes to school. Miguel's bus takes 17 more minutes to get to school. Jo's bus takes 20 more minutes to get to school. How many minutes does it take Jo's bus to get to school?

   _____ minutes

3. On what day did the art exhibit have the most visitors? Tell how you know.

   _____

   _____

   _____

   _____

Number of Visitors to the Art Exhibit			
Visitor	Friday	Saturday	Sunday
Children	21	43	19
Adults	18	51	28

4. Who visited the art exhibit more, adults or children? Tell how you know.

   _____

   _____

5-9

Skills Practice

Problem-Solving Investigation: Choose a Strategy

Choose a strategy. Solve.

Problem-Solving Strategies
• Draw a picture
• Work backward
• Write a number sentence

1. Mr. Garcia's class buys tickets for the basketball game. They buy 27 children's tickets and 35 adult tickets. The team also gives them 30 free tickets. How many tickets does the class have in all?

_____ tickets

2. At the game there are 18 band members in red. 22 band members wear blue and 31 wear white. How many band members are there in all?

_____ band members

3. At the snack stand, Tony sells 34 bags of popcorn. He sells 25 drinks and 32 hotdogs. How many snacks does he sell in all?

_____ snacks

4. Cheryl scores 28 points. Jia scores 12 points more than Cheryl does. Brooke scores 18 more points than Jia. How many points does Brooke score?

_____ points

Name _____

Reteach

Subtract Tens

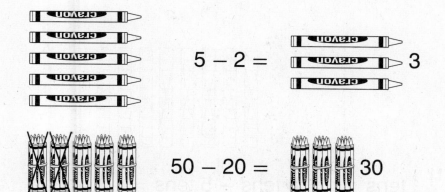

$5 - 2 =$ 3

$50 - 20 =$ 30

You can use basic facts to help subtract tens.
$5 - 2 = 3$ helps you know that $50 - 20 = 30$.

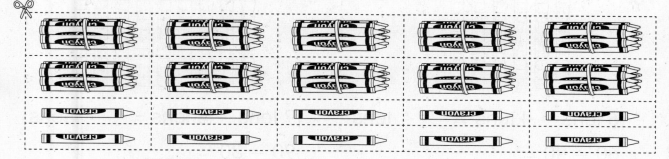

Cut out the squares. Glue them to match the problems.

1. $3 - 2 =$ _____

2. $30 - 20 =$ _____

3. $50 - 30 =$ _____

4. $40 - 10 =$ _____

5. $70 - 20 =$ _____

6. $60 - 30 =$ _____

7. $80 - 40 =$ _____

8. $90 - 10 =$ _____

Name _____

Skills Practice

Subtract Tens

Subtract tens.

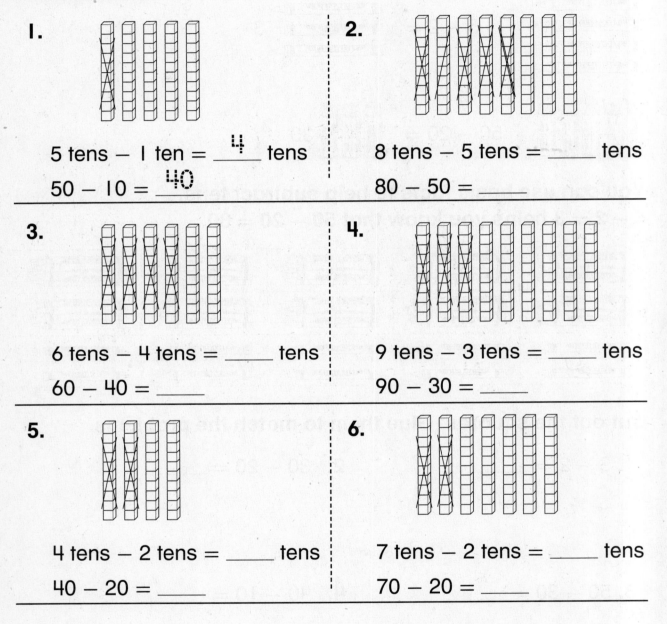

1.

5 tens − 1 ten = ___4___ tens

50 − 10 = __40__

2.

8 tens − 5 tens = _____ tens

80 − 50 = _____

3.

6 tens − 4 tens = _____ tens

60 − 40 = _____

4.

9 tens − 3 tens = _____ tens

90 − 30 = _____

5.

4 tens − 2 tens = _____ tens

40 − 20 = _____

6.

7 tens − 2 tens = _____ tens

70 − 20 = _____

Solve.

7. What is 2 tens from 7 tens? _____ − _____ = _____

8. What is 3 tens from 5 tens? _____ − _____ = _____

Name _____

Reteach

Count Back Tens and Ones

4 − 3 = ?

Count back by ones to subtract.

3, 2, 1, . . . 4 − 3 = 1

40 − 30 = ?

Count back by tens to subtract ten.

30, 20, 10 . . . 40 − 30 = 10

Subtract. Cross out the buttons as you count back. Write your answer.

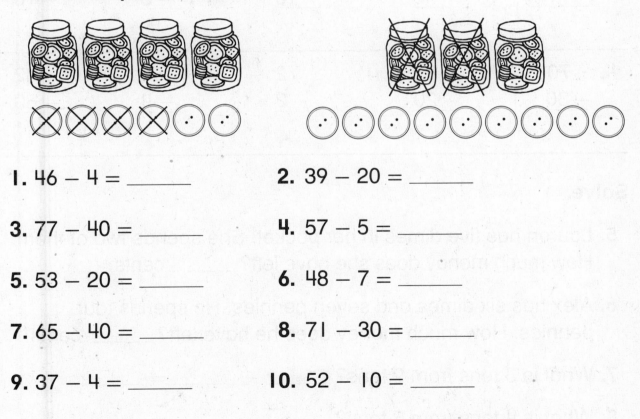

1. 46 − 4 = _____   **2.** 39 − 20 = _____

3. 77 − 40 = _____   **4.** 57 − 5 = _____

5. 53 − 20 = _____   **6.** 48 − 7 = _____

7. 65 − 40 = _____   **8.** 71 − 30 = _____

9. 37 − 4 = _____   **10.** 52 − 10 = _____

6-2

Skills Practice

Count Back Tens and Ones

Count back to subtract. Write the difference. Use ▭▭▭▭▭▭▭▭ to help.

1. 28 − 5	64 − 30	36 − 4	52 − 10	45 − 2
2. 61 − 40	68 − 2	75 − 50	89 − 20	37 − 3
3. 54 − 1	65 − 40	32 − 10	60 − 3	26 − 10
4. 70 − 30	45 − 20	72 − 2	55 − 4	82 − 60

Solve.

5. Lauren has five dimes in her pocket. She spends two of them. How much money does she have left? _____ cents

6. Alex has six dimes and seven pennies. He spends four pennies. How much money does he have left? _____ cents

7. What is 3 tens from 9 tens? _____ − _____ = _____

8. What is 4 tens from 5 tens? _____ − _____ = _____

Name _____

Reteach

Regroup Tens as Ones

Candy had 32 markers. She gives six to Ray.
How many markers does she have left?

$32 - 6 = ?$

**To help solve this problem, you can regroup one
box of markers as ten markers.**

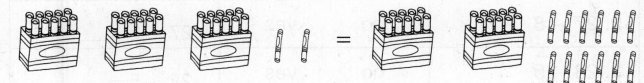

Now there are enough markers. Subtract.

$32 - 6 =$ _____. Candy has 26 markers left.

**Write the number sentences. Use ⬚⬚⬚⬚⬚⬚⬚⬚⬚.
Regroup if needed. Then solve.**

1. Jim had 52 posters. He sold 18 of them.
   How many posters does he have now?

   _____ − _____ = _____

2. Ellen had 34 crayons. She gives 5 to her friends.
   How many does she have left?

   _____ − _____ = _____

3. John had 41 pennies. He spent 15 of them.
   How many pennies does he have now?

   _____ − _____ = _____

Name _____

Skills Practice

Regroup Tens as Ones

Use WorkMat 6 and ⬚⬚⬚⬚⬚⬚⬚ **to subtract.**

	Do you need more ones to subtract?		Write the difference.
1. 32 − 5	no	yes	32 − 5 = _____
2. 27 − 8	no	yes	27 − 8 = _____
3. 28 − 5	no	yes	28 − 5 = _____
4. 55 − 7	no	yes	55 − 7 = _____
5. 41 − 6	no	yes	41 − 6 = _____
6. 36 − 9	no	yes	36 − 9 = _____

Solve.

7. Brian has 42 trading cards. He gives seven to a friend. How many trading cards does Brian have left?

_____ trading cards

8. Sam has 33 cents. He spends 15 at the store. How much money does he have left?

_____ cents

Reteach (1)

Problem-Solving Strategy: Write a Number Sentence

There are eight bats in a tower.
Three more join them.
How many bats are now in the tower?

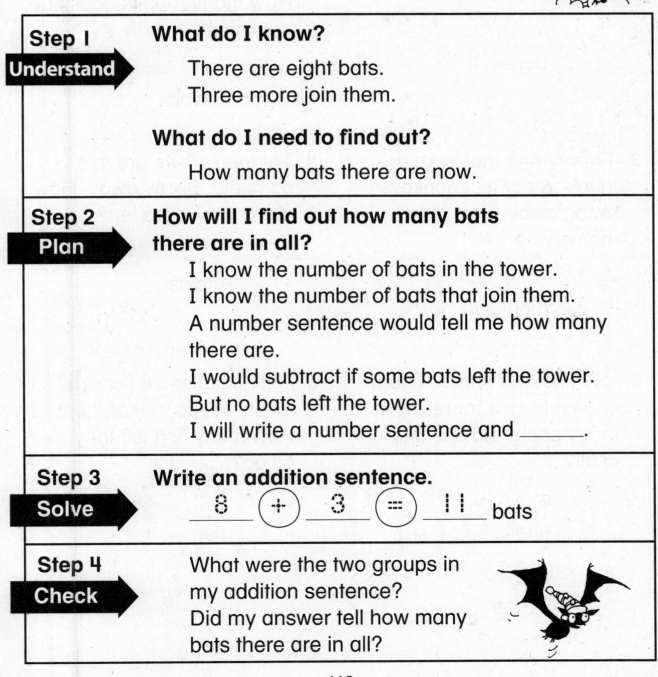

Step 1 **Understand**	**What do I know?** There are eight bats. Three more join them. **What do I need to find out?** How many bats there are now.
Step 2 **Plan**	**How will I find out how many bats there are in all?** I know the number of bats in the tower. I know the number of bats that join them. A number sentence would tell me how many there are. I would subtract if some bats left the tower. But no bats left the tower. I will write a number sentence and _____.
Step 3 **Solve**	**Write an addition sentence.** ___8___ (+) ___3___ (=) ___11___ bats
Step 4 **Check**	What were the two groups in my addition sentence? Did my answer tell how many bats there are in all?

Name _____

Reteach (2)

Problem-Solving Strategy: Write a Number Sentence

Write a number sentence to solve.

1. Spot has 13 bones in his doghouse. He found four more in the yard. How many bones does Spot have?

_____ bones

2. Lu sees 17 rabbits in a field. She sees six more in the woods.

How many rabbits does she see in all?

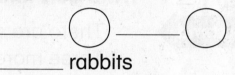

_____ rabbits

3. Twenty-one monkeys are in the tree. Five monkeys swing away. How many monkeys are left?

_____ monkeys

4. Thirteen crows are in a cornfield. Six fly away. How many crows are left?

_____ crows

5. Kay finds six shells. Then she finds nine more. How many shells did she find in all?

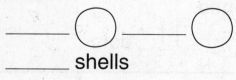

_____ shells

6. Joey catches 18 fish. His family keeps four of them. How many fish did they let go?

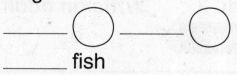

_____ fish

6-4

Skills Practice

Problem-Solving Strategy: Write a Number Sentence

Write a number sentence to solve.

1. Seven kids are in the sandbox. Six more are on the swings. How many kids are there in all?

   _____ ◯ _____ ◯

   _____ kids

2. Erica colors 15 pictures. She gives 11 to her family. How many pictures are left?

   _____ ◯ _____ ◯

   _____ pictures

3. Ben ran 11 miles. Jeff ran 5 miles. How many more miles did Ben run?

   _____ miles

4. Roland mows lawns. He made 22 dollars the first week. He made 7 dollars the next. How much money did he make?

   _____ dollars

5. Nine chickens are eating. Fourteen more chickens join them. How many chickens are eating now?

   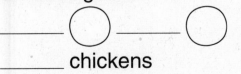

   _____ chickens

6. Jesse buys 16 game cards. He gives 4 to his friends. How many cards does Jesse have left?

   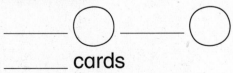

   _____ cards

Name _____

Reteach

Subtract One-Digit Numbers from Two-Digit Numbers

Find 42 − 8.

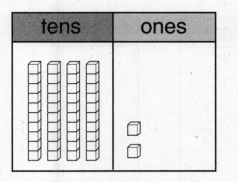

tens	ones

Show 42.
Can you subtract 8 ones?
Regroup 1 ten as 10 ones.
Now there are 3 tens and
12 ones.

$$\begin{array}{r} \boxed{3}\ \boxed{12} \\ 4\!\!\!/2 \\ -\ \ 8 \\ \hline \end{array}$$

Use WorkMat 6 and ▭▭▭▭ to subtract.

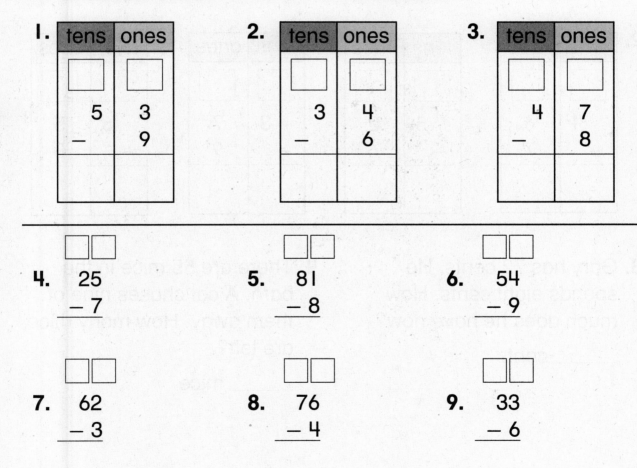

1.

tens	ones
☐	☐
5	3
−	9

2.

tens	ones
☐	☐
3	4
−	6

3.

tens	ones
☐	☐
4	7
−	8

4. ☐☐
   25
 − 7

5. ☐☐
   81
 − 8

6. ☐☐
   54
 − 9

7. ☐☐
   62
 − 3

8. ☐☐
   76
 − 4

9. ☐☐
   33
 − 6

Name _____

Skills Practice

Subtract One-Digit Numbers from Two-Digit Numbers

Use WorkMat 6 and 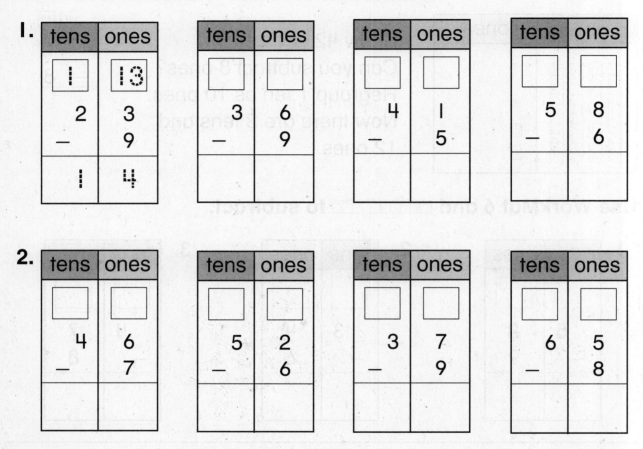 **to subtract.**

1.
tens	ones
1	13
2	3
−	9
1	4

tens	ones
3	6
−	9

tens	ones
4	1
−	5

tens	ones
5	8
−	6

2.
tens	ones
4	6
−	7

tens	ones
5	2
−	6

tens	ones
3	7
−	9

tens	ones
6	5
−	8

3. Gary has 72 cents. He spends eight cents. How much does he have now?

_____ cents

4. There are 55 mice in the barn. A cat chases nine of them away. How many mice are left?

_____ mice

Name _____

Reteach

Subtract Two-Digit Numbers

Find 36 − 17.

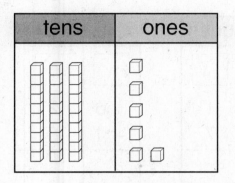

tens	ones

Show 36.
Can you subtract 7 ones?
Regroup 1 ten as 10 ones.
Now there are 2 tens and
16 ones.

$$\begin{array}{r}\boxed{2}\ \boxed{16} \\ \cancel{3}\,\cancel{6} \\ -\ 1\ 7 \\ \hline \end{array}$$

Use WorkMat 6 and ⬚⬚⬚⬚⬚⬚⬚⬚ to subtract.

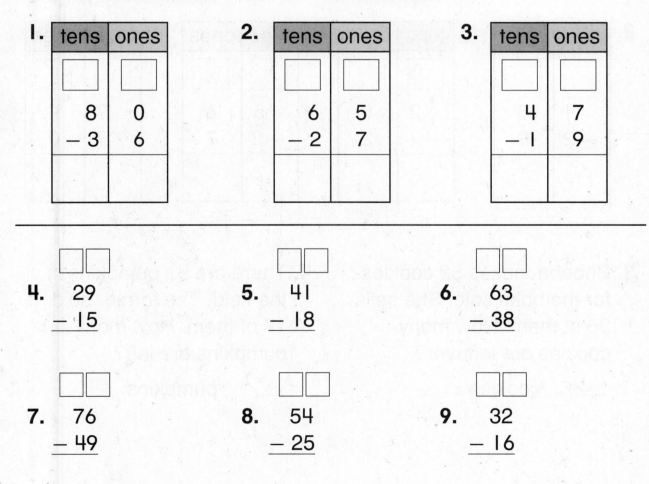

1.

tens	ones
8	0
− 3	6

2.

tens	ones
6	5
− 2	7

3.

tens	ones
4	7
− 1	9

4. 29
− 15

5. 41
− 18

6. 63
− 38

7. 76
− 49

8. 54
− 25

9. 32
− 16

Name _____

Skills Practice

Subtract Two-Digit Numbers

Use WorkMat 6 and ▭▭▭▭▭ **to subtract.**

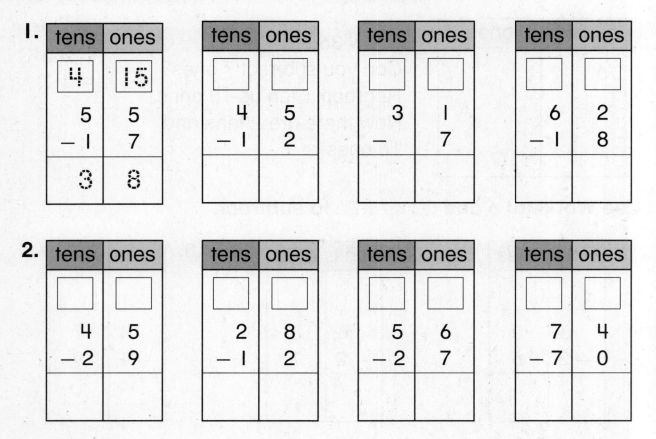

1.

tens	ones
4	15
5	5
− 1	7
3	8

tens	ones
4	5
− 1	2

tens	ones
3	1
−	7

tens	ones
6	2
− 1	8

2.

tens	ones
4	5
− 2	9

tens	ones
2	8
− 1	2

tens	ones
5	6
− 2	7

tens	ones
7	4
− 7	0

3. Phoebe makes 52 cookies for the bake sale. She sells 36 of them. How many cookies are leftover?

_____ cookies

4. There are 41 pumpkins in the field. The farmer sold 17 of them. How many pumpkins are left?

_____ pumpkins

Name _____

Reteach

Check Subtraction

Find 32 − 14.

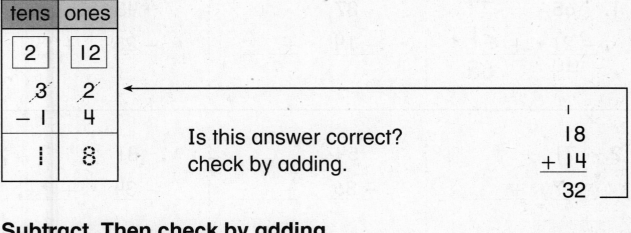

tens	ones
2	12
3	2
− 1	4
1	8

Is this answer correct?
check by adding.

$$
\begin{array}{r}
1 \\
18 \\
+ 14 \\
\hline
32
\end{array}
$$

Subtract. Then check by adding.

1.   16   11
        − 5   + 5
        ‾‾‾   ‾‾‾
         11   16

2.   53
        − 18   + 18

3.   93
        − 38   + 38

4.   46
        − 23   + 23

5.   84
        − 57   + 57

6.   75
        − 49   + 49

Name _____

Skills Practice

Check Subtraction

Subtract. Then check by adding.

1. $\begin{array}{r} 65 \\ -21 \\ \hline 44 \end{array}$ $\begin{array}{r} 44 \\ +21 \\ \hline 65 \end{array}$ $\begin{array}{r} 37 \\ -14 \\ \hline \end{array}$ $+$ ____ $\begin{array}{r} 43 \\ -25 \\ \hline \end{array}$ $+$ ____

2. $\begin{array}{r} 71 \\ -7 \\ \hline \end{array}$ $+$ ____ $\begin{array}{r} 54 \\ -36 \\ \hline \end{array}$ $+$ ____ $\begin{array}{r} 81 \\ -34 \\ \hline \end{array}$ $+$ ____

3. $\begin{array}{r} 95 \\ -23 \\ \hline \end{array}$ $+$ ____ $\begin{array}{r} 63 \\ -9 \\ \hline \end{array}$ $+$ ____ $\begin{array}{r} 48 \\ -19 \\ \hline \end{array}$ $+$ ____

Solve. Check by adding.

4. Students in Mr. Frank's class made 10 pictures. They showed 6 at the art fair. How many were not shown?

   _____ pictures

5. Mr. Levine is 53 years old. Mr. Smith is 37 years old. How much older is Mr. Levine?

   _____ years older

Name _____

Reteach (1)

Problem-Solving Investigation: Choose a Strategy

Mildred Mouse counted 18 holes in one piece of cheese. She counted 31 holes in the other piece of cheese. How many holes are there in all?

Step 1 **Understand**	**What do I know?**
	There are 18 holes in one piece of cheese. There are 31 holes in the other piece of cheese.
	What do I need to find out?
	How many holes are there?
Step 2 **Plan**	**How will I find out?**
	I can draw a picture to find out how many holes there are. But that would take a long time.
	I can write a number sentence. But it might be easier to use a model.
	I can use a model.
Step 3 **Solve**	**Use a model.**
	There are _____ holes.
Step 4 **Check**	Does my model show how many holes there are? Can I use my model to check my work?

Name _____

Reteach (2)

Problem-Solving Investigation: Choose a Strategy

Choose a strategy to solve.

Problem Solving Strategy
• Write a number sentence • Draw a picture • Use a model

1. 55 girls and 36 boys play volleyball.
How many more girls than boys
play volleyball?

_____ more girls

Show your work here.

2. There are 48 cows in the field.
There are 23 in the barn.
How many cows are there?

_____ cows

Use the chart for Exercises 3 and 4.

Swimmer	Number of Laps
Dan	22
Sandy	18
Alan	45

3. During swimming practice, how many
laps did Dan and Sandy swim?

_____ laps

4. How many more laps did Alan
swim than Sandy?

_____ laps

Name _____

Skills Practice

Problem-Solving Investigation: Choose a Strategy

Choose a strategy to solve.

Problem Solving Strategy
• Write a number sentence
• Draw a picture
• Use a model

Show your work here.

1. There are 18 frogs in the pond.
   There are five frogs in the grass.
   How many frogs are there?

   _____ frogs

2. Together, Jamie and Alex picked
   72 berries. Jamie picked 32.
   How many did Alex pick?

   _____ berries

3. There are 10 boys and 17 girls
   at the mall.
   How many kids are there?

   _____ kids

4. Ian has five sets of 10 crayons.
   He gives three crayons from
   each set to his brother.
   How many crayons does
   Ian have left?

   _____ crayons

Name _____

Reteach

Estimate Differences

In the problem below, you need to know about how many peanuts are left. You need to make a good guess. A guess is also called an estimate. You can estimate when you do not need an exact answer.

There are 18 peanuts in the pile. Edna the elephant eats 9 of them. About how many peanuts are left?

Step 1: Round each number to the nearest ten.

The number 9 is close to 10.   The number 18 is close to 20.
9 rounds to 10.   18 rounds to 20.

Step 2: Subtract the rounded numbers to find your estimate.

18 − 9 is about the same as 20 − 10.
20 − 10 = 10
18 − 9 is about _____.

Round these numbers to the nearest ten and estimate the difference.

1. $\begin{array}{r} 47 \rightarrow 50 \\ -\,31 \rightarrow -\,30 \\ \hline \end{array}$

2. $\begin{array}{r} 42 \rightarrow \\ -\,33 \rightarrow - \\ \hline \end{array}$

3. $\begin{array}{r} 39 \rightarrow \\ -\,32 \rightarrow - \\ \hline \end{array}$

4. $\begin{array}{r} 47 \rightarrow \\ -\,38 \rightarrow - \\ \hline \end{array}$

Name _____

Skills Practice

Estimate Differences

Round each number to the nearest ten. Estimate the difference.

> Round up if the number has 5, 6, 7, 8, or 9 ones.
> 15 rounds up to 20.
> Round down if the number has 4, 3, 2, or 1 ones.
> 14 rounds down to 10.

1. 49 − 31

$$\begin{array}{r} 50 \\ -\ 30 \\ \hline 20 \end{array}$$

2. 66 − 27

$$\begin{array}{r} \\ -\ \underline{} \end{array}$$

3. 77 − 31

$$-\ \underline{}$$

4. 39 − 31

$$-\ \underline{}$$

5. 48 − 32

$$-\ \underline{}$$

6. 89 − 11

$$-\ \underline{}$$

Solve.

7. Sharon spent 33 cents at the carnival. Her brother spent 19 cents. About how much more did Sharon spend?

_____ cents

8. Morgan has 32 music CDs. He gives 13 to his brother. About how many music CDs does Morgan have left?

_____ CDs

128

7-1

Reteach

Pennies, Nickels, and Dimes

You can skip count to find the value of pennies, nickels, and dimes.

penny 1¢
Count by ones.

nickel 5¢
Count by fives.

dime 10¢
Count by tens.

10,   20,   30,   40,   50

Circle the coins you need to buy the object.

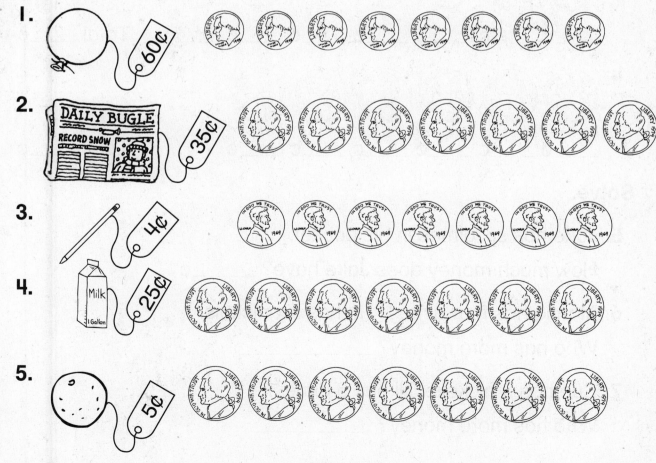

1. 60¢

2. DAILY BUGLE   RECORD SNOW   35¢

3. 4¢

4. Milk 1 Gallon   25¢

5. 5¢

7-1

Skills Practice

Pennies, Nickels, and Dimes

count to find the value.

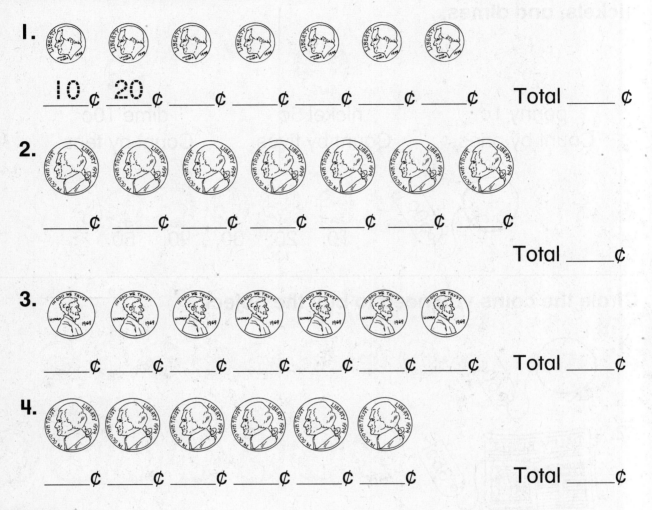

1. __10__¢ __20__¢ _____¢ _____¢ _____¢ _____¢ _____¢   Total _____¢

2. _____¢ _____¢ _____¢ _____¢ _____¢ _____¢ _____¢

   Total _____¢

3. _____¢ _____¢ _____¢ _____¢ _____¢ _____¢ _____¢   Total _____¢

4. _____¢ _____¢ _____¢ _____¢ _____¢ _____¢   Total _____¢

Solve.

5. Jake has six dimes in his pocket.

How much money does Jake have? _____¢

6. Marcia has four dimes. Tia has six nickels.

Who has more money? _____

7. Sue has 5 nickels. Jill has 5 dimes.

Who has more money? _____

Name _____

Reteach

Quarters and Half-Dollars

You can skip count to find the value of quarters and half-dollars.

quarter 25¢
Count by twenty-fives.

half-dollar 50¢
Count by fifties.

25,   50,   75

Circle the coins you need to buy the object.

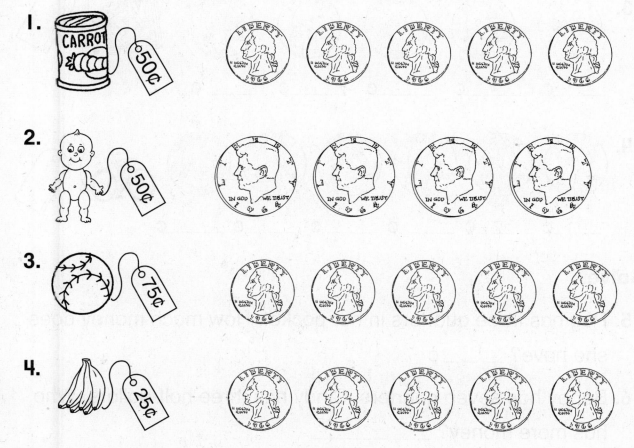

1. CARROT 50¢

2. 50¢

3. 75¢

4. 25¢

Name _____

Skills Practice

Quarters and Half-Dollars

Count to find the value of the coins. Then write the total in the price tag.

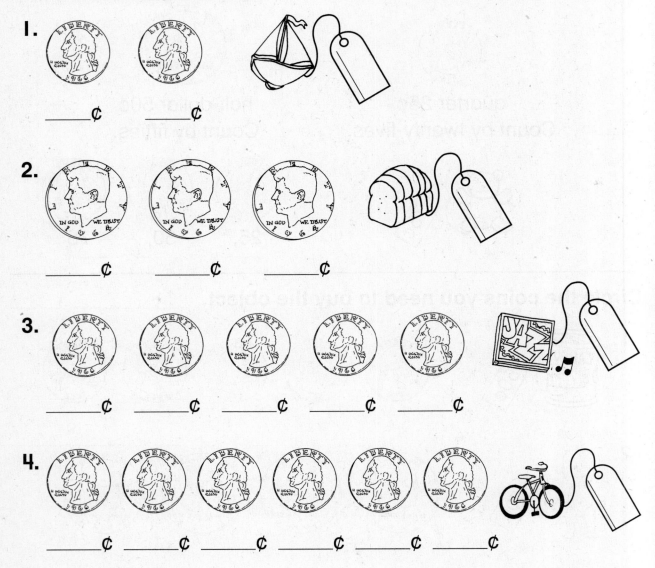

1. _____ ¢ _____ ¢

2. _____ ¢ _____ ¢ _____ ¢

3. _____ ¢ _____ ¢ _____ ¢ _____ ¢ _____ ¢

4. _____ ¢ _____ ¢ _____ ¢ _____ ¢ _____ ¢ _____ ¢

Solve.

5. Peg has three quarters in her pocket. How much money does she have? _____ ¢

6. Bobby has seven quarters. Cindy has three half-dollars. Who has more money? _____

Name _____

Reteach

Count Coins

Find the value of the coins.

__25__ ¢   __50__ ¢   __75__ ¢   __85__ ¢   total __85__ ¢

Count coins to check that there is enough money to buy the object. Circle *yes* or *no*.

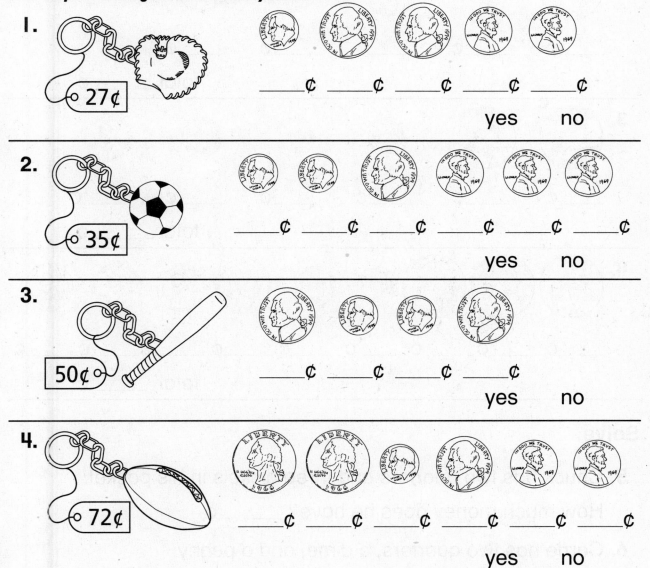

1. 27¢   ___¢ ___¢ ___¢ ___¢ ___¢

       yes   no

---

2. 35¢   ___¢ ___¢ ___¢ ___¢ ___¢ ___¢

       yes   no

---

3. 50¢   ___¢ ___¢ ___¢ ___¢

       yes   no

---

4. 72¢   ___¢ ___¢ ___¢ ___¢ ___¢ ___¢

       yes   no

7-3

Name _____

Skills Practice

Count Coins

Count to find the total amount.

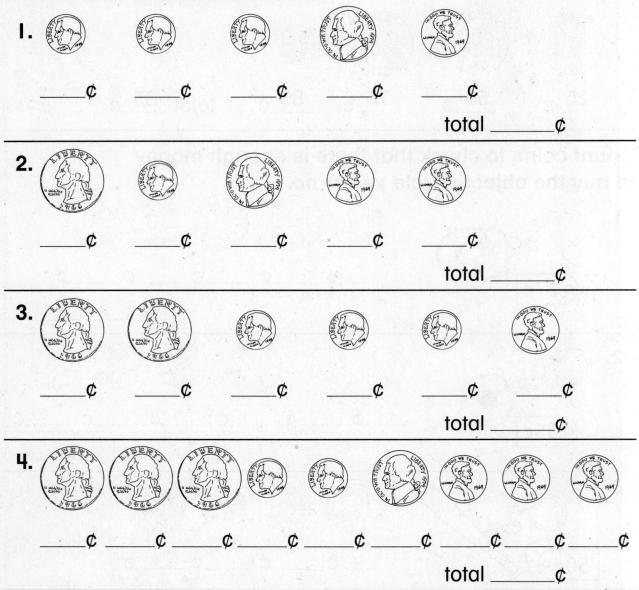

1. _____¢   _____¢   _____¢   _____¢   _____¢

   total _____¢

2. _____¢   _____¢   _____¢   _____¢   _____¢

   total _____¢

3. _____¢   _____¢   _____¢   _____¢   _____¢   _____¢

   total _____¢

4. _____¢ _____¢ _____¢ _____¢ _____¢ _____¢ _____¢ _____¢ _____¢

   total _____¢

Solve.

5. Chuck has two quarters and three nickels in his pocket.

   How much money does he have? _____¢

6. Carrie has two quarters, a dime, and a penny.

   How much money does she have? _____¢

Name _____

Reteach (1)

Problem-Solving Strategy: Act It Out

Tara has four turtles.
Each turtle cost 10 cents.
How much did Tara spend on turtles?

Step 1 **Understand**	**What do I know?** Tara has four turtles. Turtles cost 10 cents each. **What do I need to find?** How much do four turtles cost?
Step 2 **Plan**	**How will I find the cost?** I can act it out to find out how much four turtles cost.
Step 3 **Solve**	**Act it out.** Put a dime on each turtle. Then skip count by tens to count the dimes. 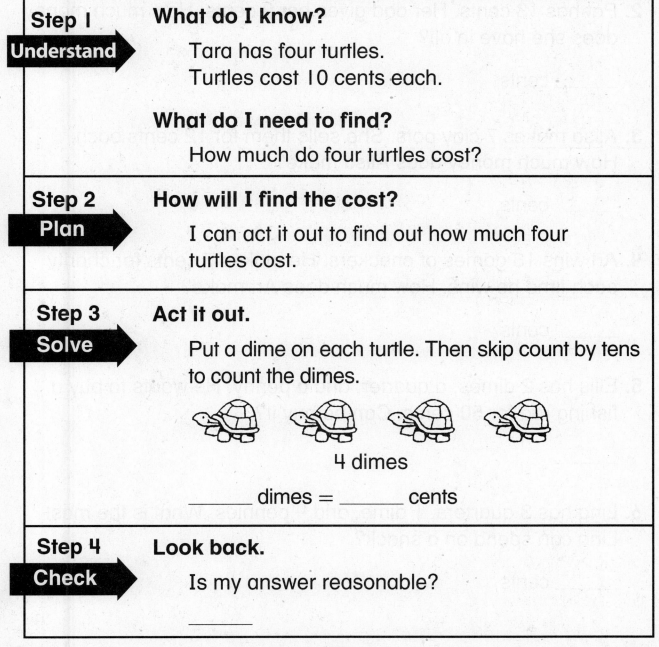 4 dimes _____ dimes = _____ cents
Step 4 **Check**	**Look back.** Is my answer reasonable? _____

Name _____

Reteach (2)

Problem-Solving Strategy: Act It Out

Use coins to act out and solve the problems.

1. Leon has 5 hermit crabs. Each costs 15 cents. How much money did Leon spend on hermit crabs?

   _____ cents

2. Pat has 13 cents. Her dad gives her 9 cents. How much money does she have in all?

   _____ cents

3. Alisa makes 7 clay pots. She sells them for 12 cents each. How much money does Alisa make?

   _____ cents

4. Art wins 13 games of checkers. He makes 7 cents for charity each time he wins. How much does Art make?

   _____ cents

5. Ellis has 2 dimes, a quarter, and a penny. He wants to buy a fishing rod for 50 cents. Can he buy it?

   _____

6. Ling has 3 quarters, 1 dime, and 4 pennies. What is the most Ling can spend on a snack?

   _____ cents

Name _____

Skills Practice

Problem-Solving Strategy: Act It Out

Use coins to act out and solve the problems.

1. Andrea has 52 cents. Her brother gives her a quarter more. How much money does Andrea have?

   _____ cents

2. Reese has 50 cents. Gary has 82 cents. How much more money does Gary have?

   _____ cents

3. Julio finds 17 cents. Luke finds 24 cents. How much more money does Luke find?

   _____ cents

4. Greg has a half-dollar in his pocket. His sister gives him a quarter and a penny. How much money does Greg have now?

   _____ cents

5. Miko has 7 pennies, 3 nickels, 1 dime, and 1 quarter. Does she have enough to buy a pen for 50 cents?

   _____

6. Nick has 85 cents. He buys a juice box for 2 dimes. How much does he have now?

   _____ cents

Name _____

Reteach

Dollar

You can use different coins to make one dollar.

100 pennies = $1.00
20 nickels = $1.00
10 dimes = $1.00
4 quarters = $1.00
2 half-dollars = $1.00
1 dollar bill = $1.00

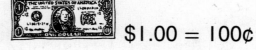

A dollar is equal to 100¢. $1.00 = 100¢

Circle the coins in each row that equal $1.00.

1.

2.

3.

4.

Name _____

Skills Practice

Dollar

Count the coins. Write the value.
Circle the coins that make one dollar.

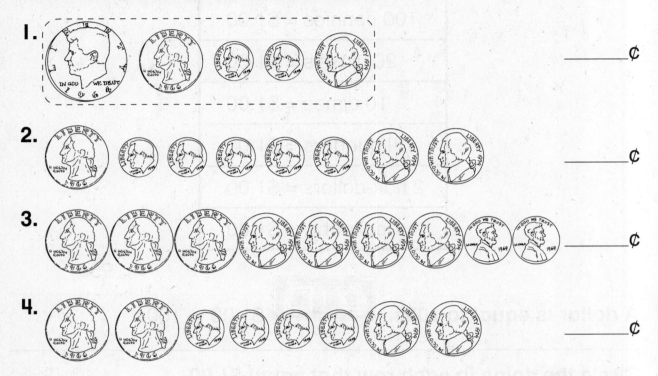

1. _____ ¢

2. _____ ¢

3. _____ ¢

4. _____ ¢

Solve.

5. It costs one dollar to ride the merry-go-round. Anna has two quarters, two dimes, five nickels, and five pennies. Does she have enough money? _____

6. Leon has three quarters, one dime, one nickel, and two pennies. A loaf of bread costs one dollar. Does Leon have enough to buy a loaf? _____

7. Sylva has four quarters, a penny, and a nickel. If she buys a puzzle for one dollar, how much will Sylva have left?

_____ ¢

Reteach

Add Money

Adding money is like adding numbers.

35¢	35		20¢	20
+ 45¢	+ 45		+ 42¢	+ 42
80¢	80		62¢	62

Remember to write the ¢ in your answer.

Add the money. Circle the answer.

1.
     27¢
    + 35¢

    52¢   62¢

2.
     13¢
    + 72¢

    85¢   95¢

3.
     84¢
    + 9¢

    93¢   83¢

4.
     46¢
    + 17¢

    53¢   63¢

5.
     19¢
    + 52¢

    71¢   70¢

6.
     38¢
    + 13¢

    41¢   51¢

7.
     93¢
    + 6¢

    98¢   99¢

8.
     47¢
    + 45¢

    82¢   92¢

9.
     38¢
    + 16¢

    54¢   64¢

10.
      66¢
    + 14¢

    70¢   80¢

Name _____

Skills Practice

Add Money

Add.

1. 32¢
    + 34¢
    ‾‾‾‾‾

2. 14¢
    + 62¢
    ‾‾‾‾‾

3. 22¢
    + 49¢
    ‾‾‾‾‾

4. 12¢
    + 37¢
    ‾‾‾‾‾

5. 33¢
    + 49¢
    ‾‾‾‾‾

6. 32¢
    + 65¢
    ‾‾‾‾‾

Solve.

7. Leroy bought a movie ticket for 75¢. He also bought a magazine for 15¢. Add to find out how much money he spent. Draw the coins for each amount.

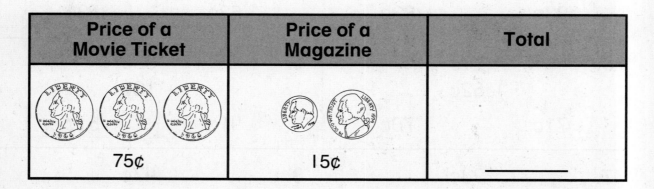

Price of a Movie Ticket	Price of a Magazine	Total
75¢	15¢	_____

8. Lee has 61¢ in her pocket. Her dad gives her 7¢. How much money does she have now? _____

9. Mr. Adler found 73¢. He had 9¢ in his pocket. How much money does he have in all? _____

7-7

Reteach

Subtract Money

Subtracting money is like subtracting numbers.

45¢	45		42¢	42
− 35¢	− 35		− 20¢	− 20
10¢	10		22¢	22

Remember to write the ¢ in your answer.

Subtract the money. Circle the answer.

1. 24¢
    − 14¢

    8¢   10¢

2. 66¢
    − 28¢

    38¢   28¢

3. 74¢
    − 32¢

    42¢   46¢

4. 91¢
    − 11¢

    70¢   80¢

5. 89¢
    − 41¢

    48¢   50¢

6. 49¢
    − 22¢

    27¢   11¢

7. 77¢
    − 69¢

    8¢   2¢

8. 96¢
    − 77¢

    19¢   24¢

9. 51¢
    − 7¢

    47¢   44¢

10. 83¢
    − 17¢

    69¢   66¢

Name _____

Skills Practice

Subtract Money

Subtract.

1. 63¢ − 41¢	2. 64¢ − 12¢	3. 94¢ − 37¢
4. 87¢ − 32¢	5. 77¢ − 41¢	6. 28¢ − 26¢

Solve.

7. Luke had 75¢. He spent 32¢. Subtract to find out how much money he has now. Draw the coins.

How Much Money Luke Had	How Much Money Luke Spent	What He Has Left
 75¢	 32¢	_____

8. Logan had 79¢ in his pocket. He spent 17¢. How much money does he have left? _____

9. Mrs. Paul gave 65¢ to her son. He spent 32¢. How much money does he have left? _____

Reteach (1)

Problem-Solving Investigation: Choose a Strategy

Joe's dad bought 20 bananas.
They ate six the first day.
How many bananas do they have left?

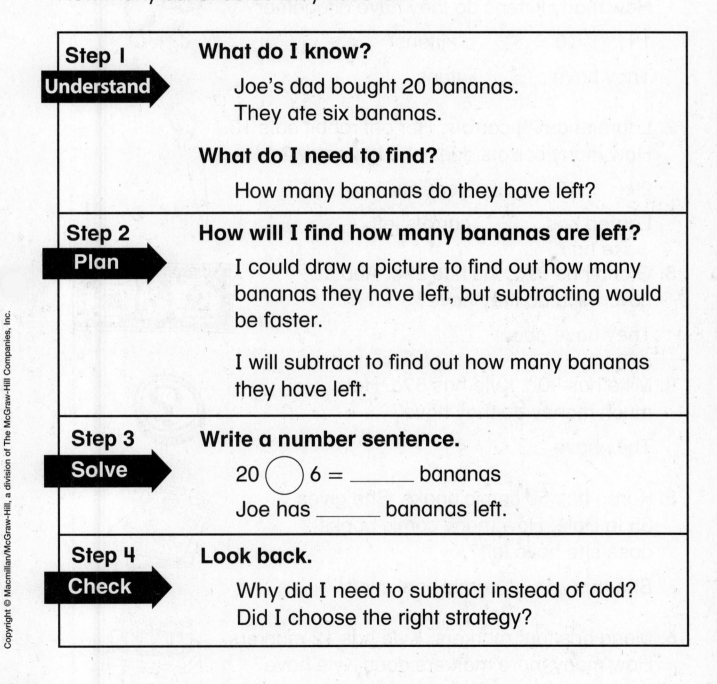

Step 1
Understand

What do I know?

Joe's dad bought 20 bananas.
They ate six bananas.

What do I need to find?

How many bananas do they have left?

Step 2
Plan

How will I find how many bananas are left?

I could draw a picture to find out how many bananas they have left, but subtracting would be faster.

I will subtract to find out how many bananas they have left.

Step 3
Solve

Write a number sentence.

20 ◯ 6 = _____ bananas
Joe has _____ bananas left.

Step 4
Check

Look back.

Why did I need to subtract instead of add?
Did I choose the right strategy?

7-8

Reteach (2)

Problem-Solving Investigation: Choose a Strategy

Choose a strategy and solve.

1. Taylor has 14 kittens. Rhonda has 10 kittens. How many kittens do they have altogether?

   14 ◯ 10 = _____ kittens

   They have _____ kittens.

2. Lauren has 24 carrots. Her pet rabbit eats 13. How many carrots does she have now?

   24 ◯ 13 = _____ carrots

   Lauren has _____ carrots left.

3. Gloria has 39¢. Vic has 24¢. About how much do they have?

   They have about _____

4. Mike has 40¢. Kyle has 59¢. How much money do they have?

   They have _____

5. Karen has 50 comic books. She gives 35 to Dale. How many comic books does she have left?

   She has _____ comic books left.

6. Maria has four markers. Kyle has 12 markers. How many more markers does Kyle have?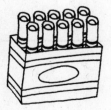

   Kyle has _____ more markers than Maria.

Name _____

Skills Practice

Problem-Solving Investigation: Choose a Strategy

Choose a strategy. Solve.

> **Problem-Solving Strategy**
> - Act it out
> - Choose an operation
> - Guess and check
> - Draw a picture

1. Mr. Gary gave his son a quarter. He gave 50¢ to his daughter. How much money did he give his children? _____

2. Amy has a quarter and four nickels. Tony has a dime and eight pennies. How much do they have altogether? _____

3. There are 13 dimes on the table. Five more dimes are in the jar. How many dimes are there in all? _____

4. Jen gets 15¢ a week for allowance. If she saves her money for four weeks, how much money will she have? _____

5. Ted has two quarters in his pocket. His friend gives him a nickel. His teacher gives him two cents. How much money does Ted have now? _____

6. Alex bought an apple for 25¢ and a banana for 16¢. Estimate how much money Alex spent. about _____

Name _____

Reteach (1)

Problem-Solving Strategy: Draw a Picture

Nina put frosting on 2 parts of a cake.
The cake has six equal parts.
What fraction of the cake has frosting?

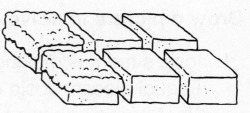

Step 1 **Understand**	**What do I know?**
	There is frosting on 2 parts of a cake. The cake has six equal parts.
	What do I need to find out?
	The fraction of the cake that has frosting.
Step 2 **Plan**	**How will I find out?**
	I can draw a picture. A picture will help me see the fractions.
Step 3 **Solve**	**Draw a picture.**
	____ of the cake has frosting.
Step 4 **Check**	**Look back.**
	How did drawing a picture help me solve the problem?

Name _____

Reteach (2)

Problem-Solving Strategy: Draw a Picture

Draw a picture to solve. Show your work.

1. Josie's mom is making a sandwich. She cuts the sandwich into 4 equal pieces. Josie eats 2 pieces. Her mom eats 1 piece. What fraction shows how much of the sandwich they eat?

   Josie and her mom eat _____ of the sandwich.

2. Tom is making a spinner for a game. He draws a circle with 6 equal parts. Then, he colors 1 part blue. What fraction of the spinner is *not* blue?

   _____ of Tom's spinner is not blue.

3. Kim and her dad are making a pizza with 8 equal slices. They put pepperoni on the first 4 slices. Then, they put peppers on the last 4 slices. Kim does not like peppers. What fraction of the pizza can she eat?

   Kim can eat _____ of the pizza.

9-3

Skills Practice

Problem-Solving Strategy: Draw a Picture

Draw a picture to solve. Show your work.

1. Ben is making a comic strip. First, he draws a rectangle with 5 equal parts. Then, Ben draws in 3 of the parts. What fraction of the comic strip did Ben draw so far?

   Ben has drawn _____ of the comic strip.

2. Jose's grandma is making a quilt. The quilt is a rectangle with 9 equal parts. 4 of the parts are green. What fraction of the quilt is green?

   _____ of the quilt is green.

3. Tina cuts a pie into 6 equal slices. She puts whipped cream on two of the slices. She leaves the other slices plain. What fraction shows how many slices are plain?

   Tina leaves _____ of the slices plain.

Name _____

Reteach

Fractions Equal to 1

There are 4 equal parts.

There are 4 shaded parts.

The number of shaded parts is the **top** *number of this fraction.* → $\frac{4}{4}$ ← *The total number of equal parts is the* **bottom** *number of a fraction.*

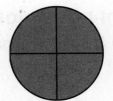

The fraction $\frac{4}{4}$ equals 1.

Count the parts in each whole.
Then write the fraction for the whole.

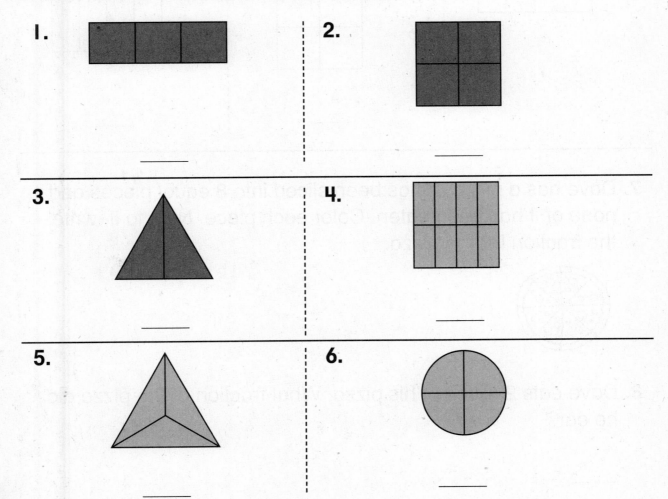

1. _____

2. _____

3. _____

4. _____

5. _____

6. _____

Name _____

Skills Practice

Fractions Equal to 1

Count and color all parts of each whole. Then write the fraction for the whole.

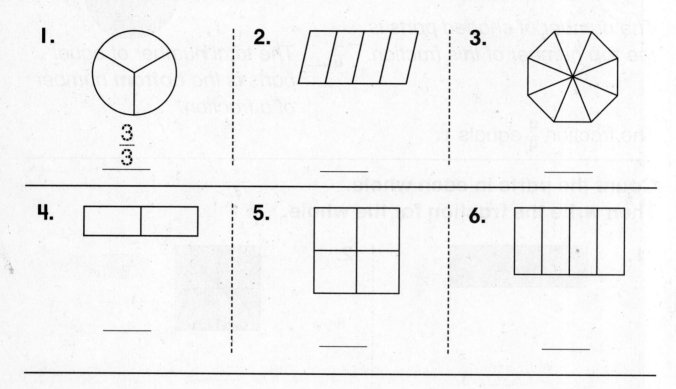

1.

$\dfrac{3}{3}$

2.

_____

3.

_____

4.

_____

5.

_____

6.

_____

7. Dave has a pizza. It has been sliced into 8 equal pieces and none of it has been eaten. Color each piece. Next to it, write the fraction for the pizza.

8. Dave eats 2 slices of his pizza. What fraction of the pizza did he eat?

_____

Name _____

Reteach

Compare Fractions

**Compare the shaded parts.
Which fraction is greater?**

$\dfrac{1}{3}$ $\dfrac{1}{2}$

**Compare the shaded parts. Then circle the
fraction that is greater.**

1.

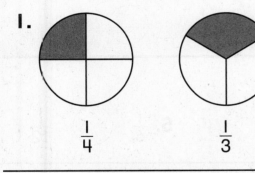   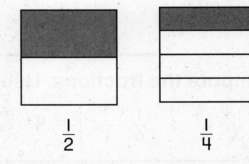

$\dfrac{1}{4}$ $\dfrac{1}{3}$ $\dfrac{1}{2}$ $\dfrac{1}{4}$

Compare the fractions. Then write < or >.

2.

$\dfrac{1}{3}$ ◯ $\dfrac{1}{6}$ $\dfrac{1}{8}$ ◯ $\dfrac{1}{4}$

3.

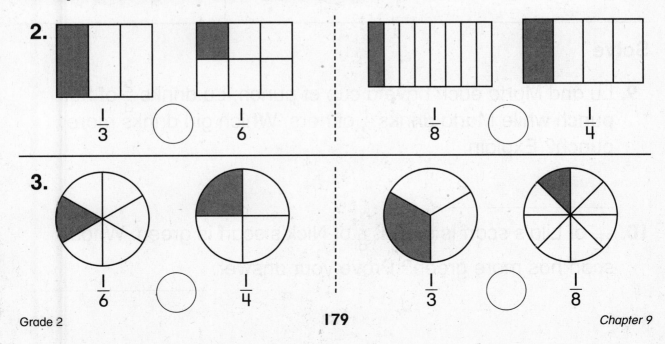

$\dfrac{1}{6}$ ◯ $\dfrac{1}{4}$ $\dfrac{1}{3}$ ◯ $\dfrac{1}{8}$

Grade 2   **179**   Chapter 9

Name _____

Skills Practice

Compare Fractions

Compare the fractions. Then write < or >.

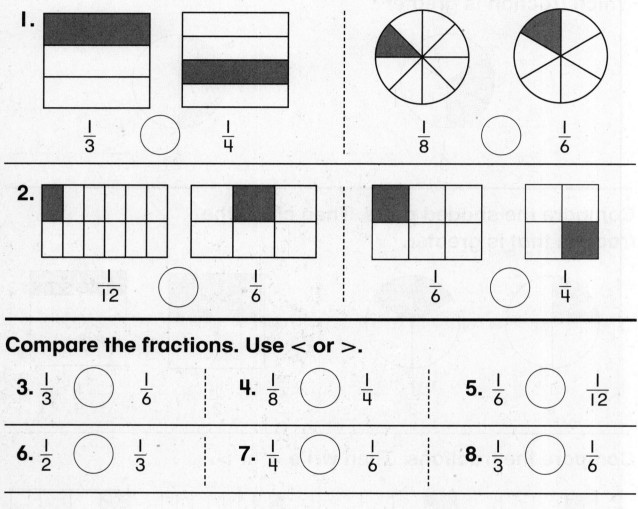

1. $\frac{1}{3}$ ◯ $\frac{1}{4}$ $\frac{1}{8}$ ◯ $\frac{1}{6}$

2. $\frac{1}{12}$ ◯ $\frac{1}{6}$ $\frac{1}{6}$ ◯ $\frac{1}{4}$

Compare the fractions. Use < or >.

3. $\frac{1}{3}$ ◯ $\frac{1}{6}$ 4. $\frac{1}{8}$ ◯ $\frac{1}{4}$ 5. $\frac{1}{6}$ ◯ $\frac{1}{12}$

6. $\frac{1}{2}$ ◯ $\frac{1}{3}$ 7. $\frac{1}{4}$ ◯ $\frac{1}{6}$ 8. $\frac{1}{3}$ ◯ $\frac{1}{6}$

Solve

9. Lu and Marta each have a cup of punch. Lu drinks $\frac{2}{3}$ of her punch while Marta drinks $\frac{1}{2}$ of hers. Which girl drinks more punch? Explain.

_____

10. $\frac{1}{12}$ of Lila's scarf is green. $\frac{1}{8}$ of Nick's scarf is green. Whose scarf has more green? Prove your answer.

_____

Name _____

Reteach

Unit Fractions of a Group

You can show a fraction of a group.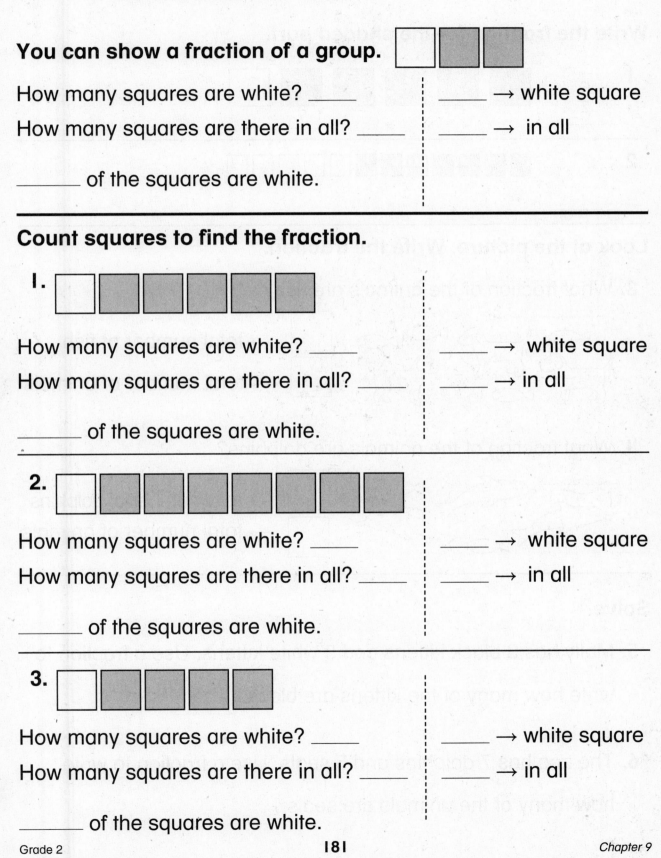

How many squares are white? _____   _____ → white square

How many squares are there in all? _____   _____ → in all

_____ of the squares are white.

Count squares to find the fraction.

1.

How many squares are white? _____   _____ → white square

How many squares are there in all? _____   _____ → in all

_____ of the squares are white.

2.

How many squares are white? _____   _____ → white square

How many squares are there in all? _____   _____ → in all

_____ of the squares are white.

3.

How many squares are white? _____   _____ → white square

How many squares are there in all? _____   _____ → in all

_____ of the squares are white.

9-6

Skills Practice

Unit Fractions of a Group

Write the fraction for the shaded part.

1. $\frac{5}{6}$

2.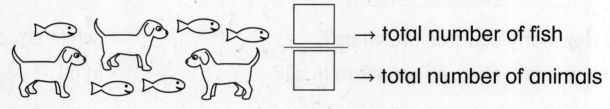

_____

Look at the picture. Write the fraction.

3. What fraction of the animals are fish?

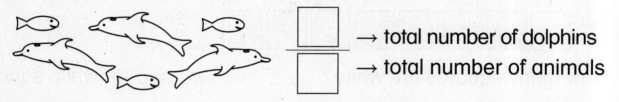

□ → total number of fish

―――

□ → total number of animals

4. What fraction of the animals are dolphins?

□ → total number of dolphins

―――

□ → total number of animals

Solve.

5. Molly has 3 black kittens and 5 white kittens. Use a fraction to write how many of the kittens are black. _____

6. The zoo has 7 dolphins and 5 seals. Use a fraction to write how many of the animals are seals. _____

Name _____

Reteach

Other Fractions of a Group

A fraction can name part of a group.

Circle the equal parts.

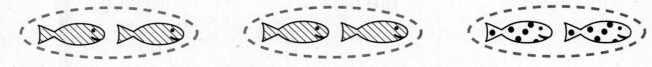

There are _____ equal parts.

What fraction of the fish are striped?

_____ of 3 equal parts are striped.

The striped part is _____ of the group.

Circle the equal parts. Then write the fraction for the striped part.

1.

_____

2.

_____

3.

_____

4.

_____

Name _____

Skills Practice

Other Fractions of a Group

Color to show the fraction of the group.

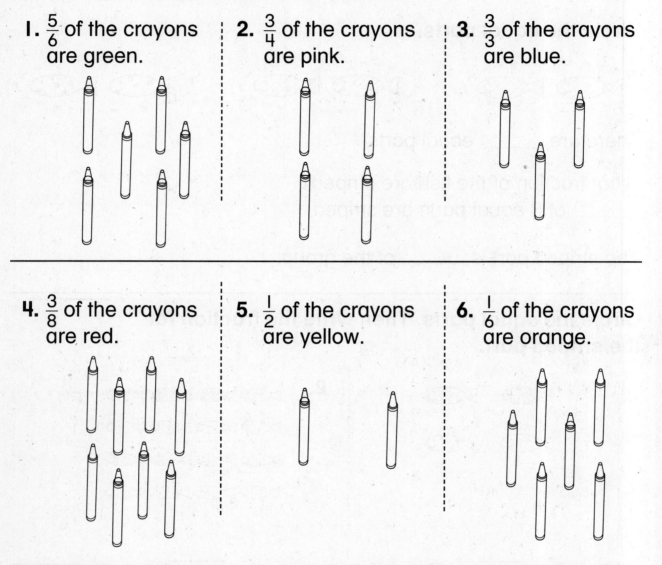

1. $\frac{5}{6}$ of the crayons are green.

2. $\frac{3}{4}$ of the crayons are pink.

3. $\frac{3}{3}$ of the crayons are blue.

4. $\frac{3}{8}$ of the crayons are red.

5. $\frac{1}{2}$ of the crayons are yellow.

6. $\frac{1}{6}$ of the crayons are orange.

Solve.

7. Eric has three black dogs and one spotted dog. Write the fraction for the black dogs.

_____

9-8

Reteach (I)

Problem-Solving Investigation: Choose a Strategy

Lin and her mom are buying eight pies.
5 of the pies are banana and the rest are apple.
What part of the pies are apple?
Show your answer as a fraction.

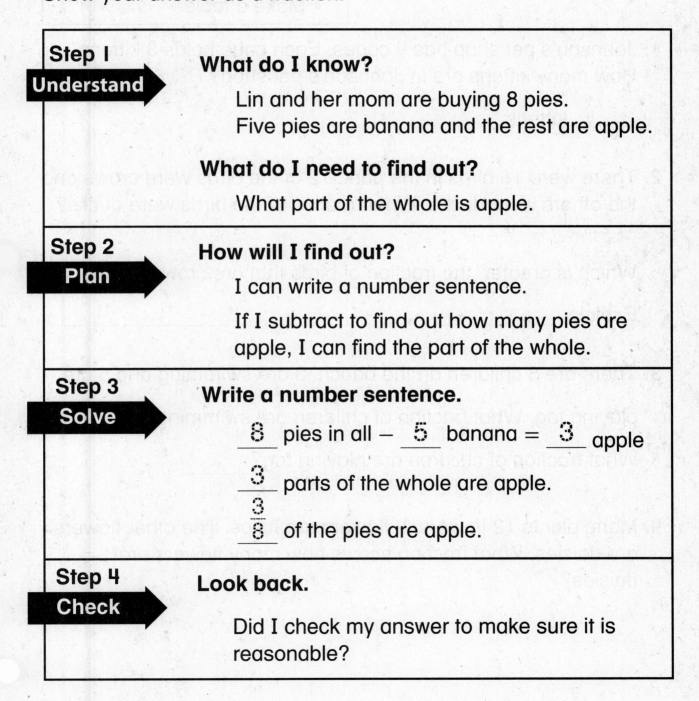

Step 1
Understand

What do I know?

Lin and her mom are buying 8 pies.
Five pies are banana and the rest are apple.

What do I need to find out?

What part of the whole is apple.

Step 2
Plan

How will I find out?

I can write a number sentence.

If I subtract to find out how many pies are apple, I can find the part of the whole.

Step 3
Solve

Write a number sentence.

___8___ pies in all − ___5___ banana = ___3___ apple

___3___ parts of the whole are apple.

$\dfrac{3}{8}$ of the pies are apple.

Step 4
Check

Look back.

Did I check my answer to make sure it is reasonable?

Name _____

Reteach (2)

Problem-Solving Investigation: Choose a Strategy

Choose a strategy to solve.

Problem-Solving Strategies
• Use a pattern
• Write a number sentence
• Make a table

1. Johnson's pet shop has 4 cages. Each cage holds 3 kittens. How many kittens are in Johnson's pet shop?

   _____ kittens

2. There were 16 birds in the park. 12 of the birds were crows and the others were ducks. What fraction of the birds were ducks?

   _____

   Which is greater, the fraction of birds that are crows or ducks?

   Explain. _____

3. There are 8 children on the beach. 3 are swimming and 5 are playing tag. What fraction of children are swimming? _____

   What fraction of children are playing tag? _____

4. Marie plants 12 flowers. 4 flowers are tulips. The other flowers are daisies. What fraction shows how many flowers are daisies?

   _____

9-8

Skills Practice

Problem-Solving Investigation: Choose a Strategy

Choose a strategy to solve.

| **Problem-Solving Strategies** |
| • Use a pattern |
| • Write a number sentence |
| • Make a table |

1. David has 12 fish. 4 of his fish are yellow and 4 are orange. How many spotted fish does David have?

   _____ spotted fish

2. Alma cut a melon in halves. She shared $\frac{1}{2}$ with her brother. Her grandparents shared the rest. How much of the

   melon did Alma eat? _____

3. Megan breaks a muffin into 3 equal pieces. She eats 2 pieces. What fraction of the muffin did she eat?

   _____

4. Juan buys 15 marbles to give to friends. He gives 5 marbles to Abby. He gives 6 marbles to Lou. He gives the rest to Jon. What fraction shows how many marbles Jon has?

   _____

5. Eve has 13 strawberries. She puts 9 in a tart. She eats the rest. How many strawberries does Eve eat?

   _____ strawberries

10-1

Reteach

Hundreds

Cut the tens and hundreds below. Glue to show the number.

1. 4 tens = 40 ones

2. 6 tens = 60 ones

3. 2 hundreds = 20 tens = 200 ones

4. 3 hundreds = 30 tens = 300 ones

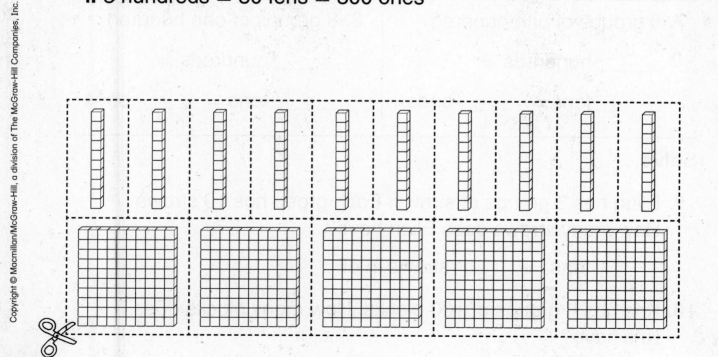

189

Name _____

Skills Practice

Hundreds

Write how many.

1. 6 groups of ten

   __6__ tens = __60__ ones

2. 9 groups of ten

   __9__ tens = _____ ones

3. 4 groups of one hundred

   _____ hundreds =

   _____ tens = _____ ones

4. 2 groups of one hundred

   _____ hundreds =

   _____ tens = _____ ones

5. 7 groups of one hundred

   _____ hundreds =

   _____ tens = _____ ones

6. 1 group of one hundred

   _____ hundred =

   _____ tens = _____ ones

7. 5 groups of one hundred

   _____ hundreds =

   _____ tens = _____ ones

8. 8 groups of one hundred

   _____ hundreds =

   _____ tens = _____ ones

Solve.

9. Elian has 3 groups of straws. Each group has 10 straws. How many straws does Elian have?

   _____ tens = _____ straws in all

10. Kris has 4 groups of 100 blocks. How many blocks does Kris have?

    _____ hundreds = _____ tens = _____ blocks in all

Name _____

Reteach

Hundreds, Tens, and Ones

You can use pictures to represent hundreds, tens, and ones.

126	__1__ hundred	__2__ tens	__6__ ones

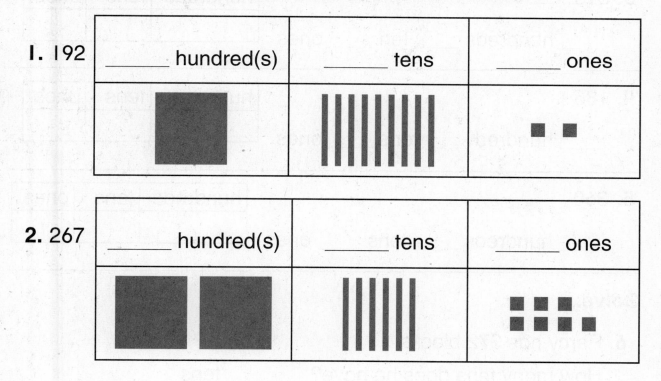

Write and draw how many hundreds, tens, and ones.

1. 192	_____ hundred(s)	_____ tens	_____ ones

2. 267	_____ hundred(s)	_____ tens	_____ ones

Write the number.

3. 3 hundreds 2 tens 5 ones = _____

4. 2 hundreds 4 tens 9 ones = _____

5. 8 hundreds 7 tens 0 ones = _____

Name _____

Skills Practice

Hundreds, Tens, and Ones

Write how many hundreds, tens, and ones.

1. 736

____7____ hundreds ____3____ tens ____6____ ones

hundreds	tens	ones
7	3	6

2. 263

____ hundreds ____ tens ____ ones

hundreds	tens	ones

3. 518

____ hundreds ____ ten ____ ones

hundreds	tens	ones

4. 185

____ hundred ____ tens ____ ones

hundreds	tens	ones

5. 360

____ hundreds ____ tens ____ ones

hundreds	tens	ones

Solve.

6. Percy has 372 blocks.

How many tens does he have? _____ tens

7. Luis has 613 beads.

How many hundreds does he have? _____ hundreds

8. Dana has 490 stickers.

How many tens does she have? _____ tens

Name _____

Reteach (1)

Problem-Solving Strategy: Make a List

Each roller coaster car seats 3 children.
Will, Mateo, and Li want to sit in the same car.
How many different ways can they sit?

Step 1 Understand	**What do I know?**
	There are 3 children.
	Their names are Will, Mateo, and Li.
	They want to sit in the same car.
	What do I need to find?
	How many different ways can they sit?
Step 2 Plan	**How will I find my answer?**
	I will make a list of all ways to sit.
	A list is a clear way to show names or numbers.
Step 3 Solve	**Make a list.**
	Will, Mateo, Li Mateo, Will, Li Li, Will, Mateo
	Will, Li, Mateo Mateo, Li, Will Li, Mateo, Will
	There are ___6___ ways to sit.
Step 4 Check	**Look back.**
	How can I be sure that I found all ways to sit?
	_____

Name _____

Reteach (2)

Problem-Solving Strategy: Make a List

Make a list to solve. Show your work.

1. Three students are running a race. Each student is wearing a number: 4, 5, or 6. The students can finish first, middle, or last. Use the numbers to find out how many ways the race can end.

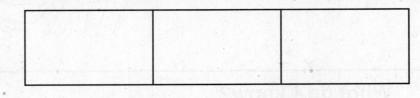

There are _____ ways for the race to end.

2. Olive is coloring 3 flowers in a row. She is using her blue, yellow, and red crayons. How many ways can she color the flowers?

There are _____ ways to color the flowers.

3. Abdul has tomato seeds and pepper seeds. He can put each in a clay pot or a plastic pot. How many different plant pots can he make?

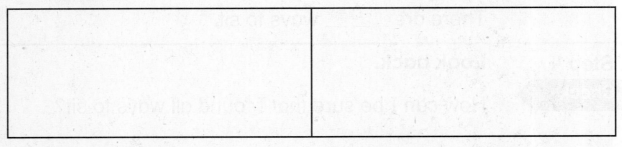

Abdul can make _____ different plant pots.

Name _____

Skills Practice

Problem-Solving Strategy: Make a List

Make a list to solve. Use a separate piece of paper.

1. Chen chooses where people sit at the picnic. He has 3 seats in a row for Mom, Lien, and Roy. How many different ways can they sit? Write them.

   _____

   _____

   _____

   They can sit in _____ different ways.

2. Nina is making a birdhouse. Birdhouse kits come in 3 sizes: big, medium, and small. She can choose from white, blue, or pink paint. How many different birdhouses can Nina make?

   Nina can make _____ different birdhouses.

3. A kite tail has space for 3 bows. Rob has a green bow, a blue bow, and a gold bow. How many different ways can Rob tie the bows?

   Rob can tie the bows in _____ different ways.

4. Lupé lost her classroom number. She remembers that it has the numbers 2, 3, and 4. How many different three-digit numbers could she try?

   Write them. _____, _____, _____, _____, _____, _____

   Lupé could try _____ rooms.

Name _____

Reteach

Place Value to 1,000

Expanded form shows how many thousands, hundreds, tens, and ones.
Match each number to the correct expanded form.

1. 345	900 + 10 + 5
2. 721	200 + 70 + 8
3. 166	700 + 20 + 1
4. 915	800 + 30 + 7
5. 584	300 + 40 + + 5
6. 439	600 + 90 + 0
7. 278	100 + 60 + 6
8. 690	1000 + 0 + 0 + 0
9. 837	500 + 80 + 4
10. 1,000	400 + 30 + 9

Name _____

Skills Practice

Place Value to 1,000

Write how many thousands, hundreds, tens, and ones. Then write the number.

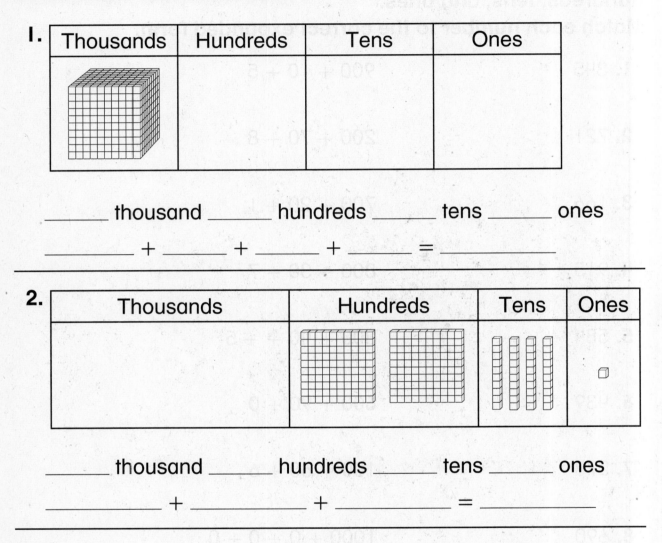

1.

Thousands	Hundreds	Tens	Ones

_____ thousand _____ hundreds _____ tens _____ ones

_____ + _____ + _____ + _____ = _____

2.

Thousands	Hundreds	Tens	Ones

_____ thousand _____ hundreds _____ tens _____ ones

_____ + _____ + _____ = _____

Solve.

3. The theater sells 142 tickets. Show how many tickets were sold in expanded form.

_____ + _____ + _____ = 142 tickets

4. An airplane flies 640 miles. How many hundreds?

_____ hundreds

10-5

Reteach

Read and Write Numbers to 1,000

Words can tell numbers.
Cut and glue words to match the numbers.

1. 496

2. 937

3. 1,000

4. 188

5. 350

6. 625

✂

one hundred eighty-eight	one thousand
four hundred ninety-six	three hundred fifty
nine hundred thirty-seven	six hundred twenty-five

10-5

Skills Practice

Read and Write Numbers to 1,000

Read the number. Write it in 2 different ways.

1. 300 + 70 + 2

   _____

hundreds	tens	ones

2. eight hundred forty-one

   _____ + _____ + _____ = _____

hundreds	tens	ones

Circle the correct number word.

3. 975

   nine hundred fifty-seven

   nine hundred seventy-five

4. 193

   one hundred ninety-three

   one hundred ninety

Solve.

5. There are 429 students at Linden School. Cora wants to write the number in words for a newsletter. What should she write?

   _____ students

6. Marco lives at nine hundred thirty-one Maple Street. Use expanded form to show Marco's address.

   _____ + _____ + _____ = _____ Maple Street

Name _____

Reteach (1)

Problem-Solving Investigation: Choose a Strategy

The bakers at Barry's Bakery baked 238 bagels.
Then, they baked 20 more bagels.
Write the number name for the number of bagels baked in all.

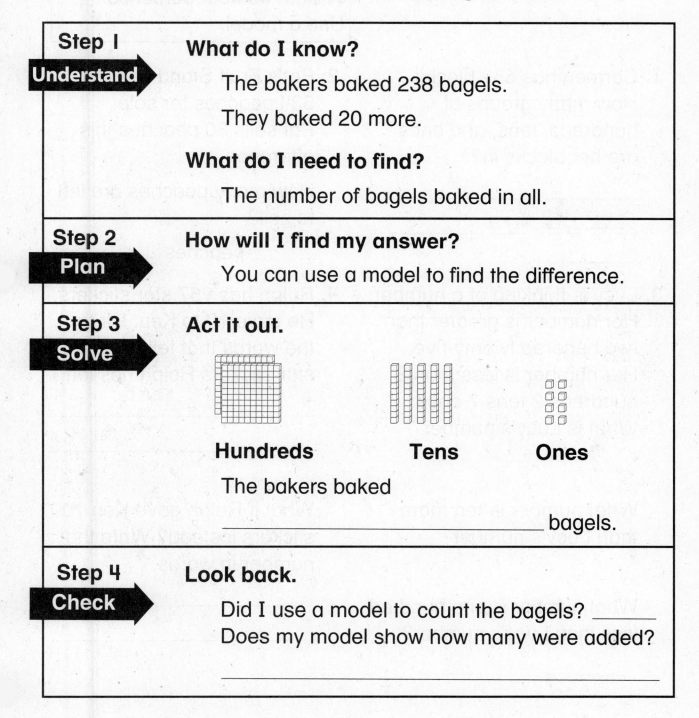

Step 1

Understand

What do I know?

The bakers baked 238 bagels.

They baked 20 more.

What do I need to find?

The number of bagels baked in all.

Step 2

Plan

How will I find my answer?

You can use a model to find the difference.

Step 3

Solve

Act it out.

Hundreds   **Tens**   **Ones**

The bakers baked

_____ bagels.

Step 4

Check

Look back.

Did I use a model to count the bagels? _____
Does my model show how many were added?

_____

10-6

Reteach (2)

Problem-Solving Investigation: Choose a Strategy

Choose a strategy. Solve.

Problem-Solving Strategies
Make an organized list
Write a number sentence
Use a model

1. Carmen has 659 blocks.
How many groups of
hundreds, tens, and ones
are her blocks in?

_____

_____

2. Pat's Fruit Stand has
534 peaches for sale.
Pat sells 30 peaches this
afternoon.

How many peaches are left
to sell?

_____ peaches

3. Lucy is thinking of a number.
Her number is greater than
two hundred twenty-five.
Her number is less than 2
hundreds 2 tens 7 ones.
What is Lucy's number?

_____

What number is ten more
than Lucy's number?

_____

What number is one hundred
less than Lucy's number?

_____

4. Ralph has 957 star stickers.
He gave 10 to Ken. Write
the words that tell how many
star stickers Ralph has left.

_____

_____

What if Ralph gave Ken 100
stickers instead? Write that
number in words.

_____

_____

10-6

Skills Practice

Problem-Solving Investigation: Choose a Strategy

Choose a strategy. Solve.

Problem-Solving Strategies
Make an organized list
Write a number sentence
Use a model

1. Naomi is playing a word game. She must write down how many ways to combine the letters N, O, and T. How many ways are there?

   There are _____ ways for Naomi to combine N, O, and T.

2. Maria's bean jar has less than 734 beans. The jar has greater than 732 beans. What is the number word for how many beans in Maria's jar?

   _____

   _____ beans

3. Franklin writes the number word four hundred ninety-one. If he shows the number in cubes, how many tens will there be? _____

4. Jin's family brings three hundred twenty-five tarts to the bake sale. They sell ten this morning. How many tarts are left to sell? _____

10-7

Reteach

Compare Numbers

Pictures can show how some numbers are greater than others.

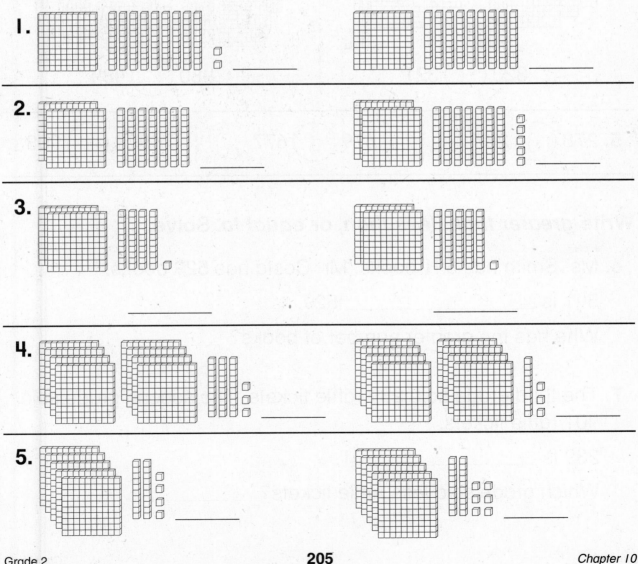

217

(221)

Look at each picture. Write the number that shows how many cubes. Then, circle the number that is greater.

1. _____   _____

2. _____   _____

3. _____   _____

4. _____   _____

5. _____   _____

Name _____

Skills Practice

Compare Numbers

Compare. Write >, <, =.

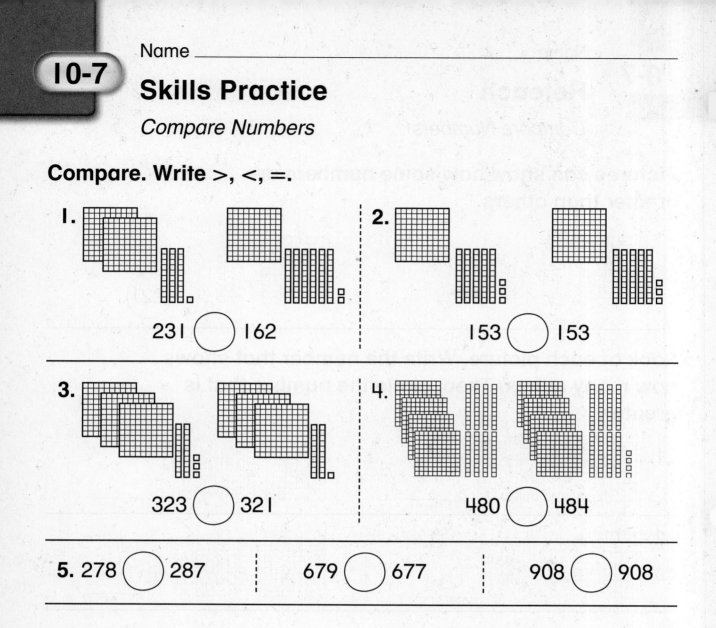

1. 231 $\bigcirc$ 162

2. 153 $\bigcirc$ 153

3. 323 $\bigcirc$ 321

4. 480 $\bigcirc$ 484

5. 278 $\bigcirc$ 287   679 $\bigcirc$ 677   908 $\bigcirc$ 908

Write *greater than*, *less than*, or *equal to*. Solve.

6. Ms. Smith has 541 books. Mr. Costa has 529 books.

   541 is _____ 529.

   Who has the greater number of books? _____

7. The third grade sold 239 raffle tickets. The second grade sold 401 raffle tickets.

   239 is _____ 401.

   Which grade sold less raffle tickets? _____

Name _____

Reteach

Order Numbers

**Place value can help order numbers
from *greatest* to *least*.**

823, 832, 932   First, compare hundreds.

932, ___, ___   932 is greater than 823 and 832.

932, 832, 823.   Then, compare tens. 832 is greater than 823.

**Write the numbers from *greatest* to *least*. Use
place value to order the numbers.**

1. 602, 612, 206

   _____, _____, _____

2. 879, 897, 987

   _____, _____, _____

3. 301, 130, 103

   _____, _____, _____

4. 455, 545, 544

   _____, _____, _____

5. 728, 287, 872

   _____, _____, _____

6. 139, 109, 301, 391

   _____, _____, _____, _____

7. 217, 720, 721, 127

   _____, _____, _____, _____

Name _____

Skills Practice

Order Numbers

Order the numbers from *greatest* to *least*.

1. 354, 674, 359   _____674_____, _____, _____

2. 592, 952, 951   _____, _____, _____

3. 808, 873, 782   _____, _____, _____

Order the numbers from *least* to *greatest*.

4. 423, 444, 324   _____, _____, _____

5. 192, 157, 132   _____, _____, _____

6. 745, 867, 748   _____, _____, _____

7. 168, 186, 166   _____, _____, _____

Solve.

8. Sen's 4 friends live on the same street. She writes down their house numbers.

234   1423   324   403

How can Sen write the house numbers from *greatest* to *least*?

_____, _____, _____, _____

9. Now Sen wants to write the house numbers from *least* to *greatest*. What should the second house number be? _____

Name _____

Reteach

Number Patterns

You can use number patterns to help you count.

Count by tens.

340, 350, _____, 370, _____, 390

Count by hundreds.

400, 500, 600, _____, 800, _____

Write the missing numbers.
Then circle the counting pattern.   **Pattern—Count by:**

1. 220, 230, _____, 250, _____, 270, 280	tens hundreds
2. 510, 520, 530, _____, 550, _____, 570	tens hundreds
3. 135, 145, 155, _____, 175, _____, 195	tens hundreds
4. 747, 757, _____, _____, 787, 797, 807	tens hundreds
5. 200, 300, 400, _____, 600, _____, 800	tens hundreds
6. 350, 450, 550, _____, _____, 850, 950	tens hundreds
7. 182, _____, 382, 482, _____, 682, 782	tens hundreds

Name _____

Skills Practice

Number Patterns

Write the missing numbers. Then write the pattern.

1. 715, 725, __735__, 745, __755__

   Each number is _____.

2. 491, _____, 691, _____, 891

   Each number is _____.

3. _____, 839, _____, 837, 836

   Each number is _____.

4. _____, 595, 495, 395, _____

   Each number is _____.

5. 599, 589, 579, _____, _____

   Each number is _____.

Use the pattern to solve.

6. The numbers have fallen off of two houses on Ivy Street. Write the missing house numbers.

   345, 355, _____, 375, _____, 395.

7. Five students are lined up for a race. Each student is wearing a number. Which students are missing?

   708, 608, 508, _____, 308, _____

Name _____

Reteach

Three-Dimensional Figures

Color each figure the correct color.

1. Color the **cone** red.

2. Color the **pyramid** blue.

3. Color the **sphere** green.

4. Color the **cube** yellow.

5. Color the **cylinder** purple.

6. Color the **rectangular prism** orange.

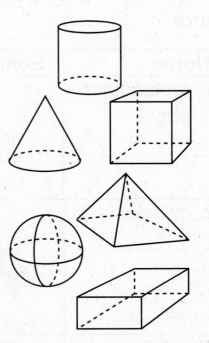

---

7. Draw a yellow line around the cone. Then draw a red line around the sphere.

8. Find the cubes in the picture. Draw a line around them.

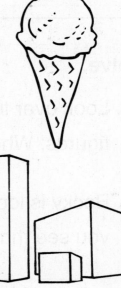

Name _____

Skills Practice

Three-Dimensional Figures

Circle the three-dimensional figure. Write the name of something in your classroom or outside that is this figure.

Name	Solid Figure	
1. rectangular prism		_____ _____
2. cylinder		_____ _____
3. cube		_____ _____

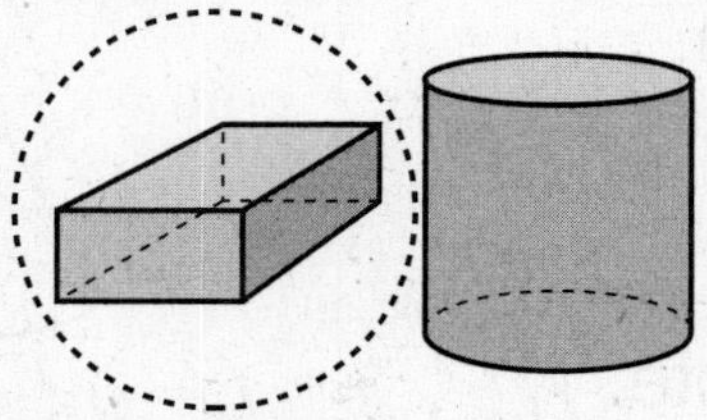

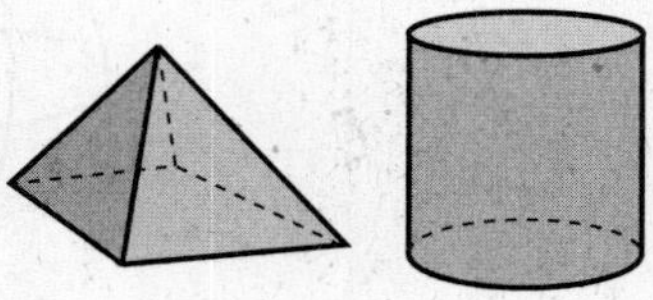

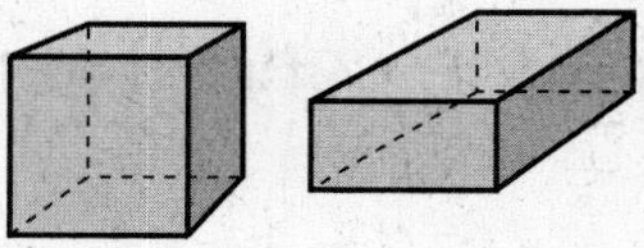

Solve.

4. Look over this page. Ryan's soup can looks like one of these figures. What figure is Ryan's soup can? _____

5. Becky is looking for figures that can stack. What figures do you see that can stack? _____

_____

Name _____

Reteach

Faces, Edges, and Vertices

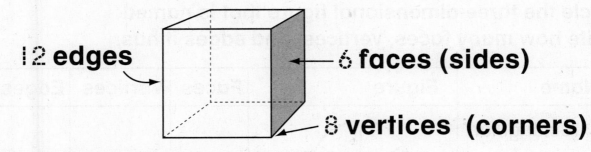

12 edges — 6 faces (sides)

8 vertices (corners)

Write how many faces, vertices, and edges.

	Solid Figure	Faces	Vertices	Edges
1.				
2.				

3. Find the figure that has one face and a point. Color it blue.

4. Find the figures with the same number of faces. Color them red.

5. Circle the figures that can roll.

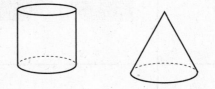

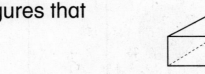

Skills Practice

Faces, Edges, and Vertices

Circle the three-dimensional figure that is named. Write how many faces, vertices, and edges it has.

Name	Figure	Faces	Vertices	Edges
1. rectangular prism		6	8	
2. cone				
3. cube				
4. pyramid				
5. sphere				

11-3

Reteach

Two-Dimensional Figures

A plane shape is a two-dimensional figure with only length and width.

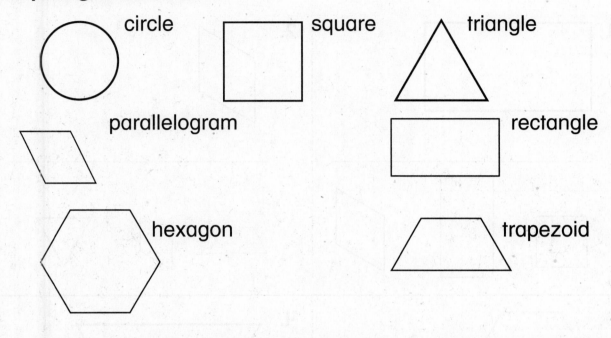

circle   square   triangle

parallelogram   rectangle

hexagon   trapezoid

Draw a line from the figure to its name.

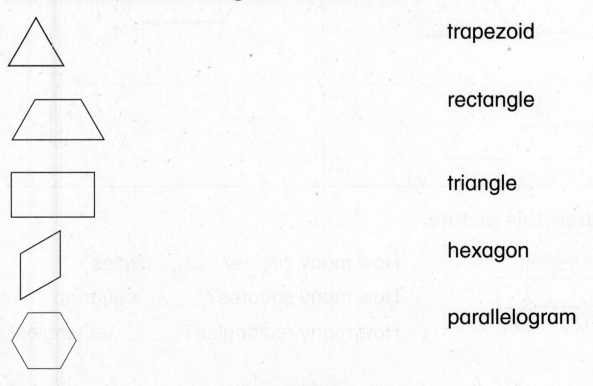

trapezoid

rectangle

triangle

hexagon

parallelogram

Name _____

Skills Practice

Two-Dimensional Figures

Write the name of the figure. Then circle the object that matches the figure.

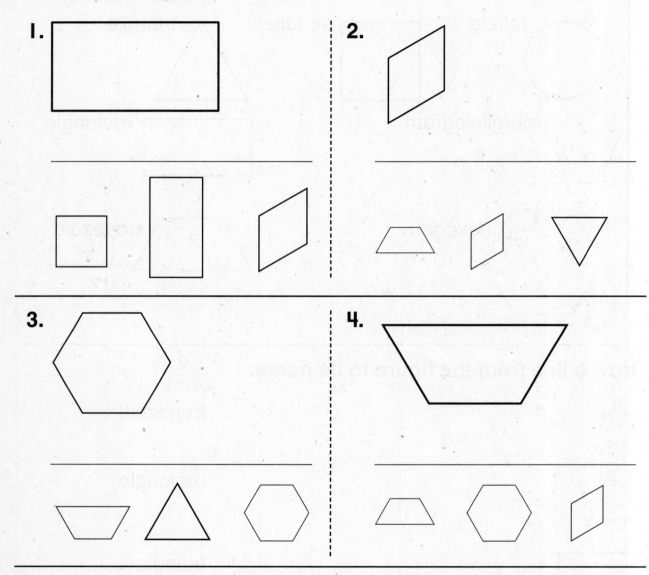

1.

_____

2.

_____

3.

_____

4.

_____

Pat drew this picture.

5.

How many circles? _____ circles

How many squares? _____ squares

How many rectangles? _____ rectangles

Reteach (1)

Problem-Solving Strategy: Look for a Pattern

Dee is making a pattern out of blocks.
She places a cone, a cube, a pyramid, a cone, and a cube.
What block comes next?

Step 1 **Understand**	**What do I know?** Dee made a pattern. She used a cone, a cube, a pyramid, a cone, and a cube. **What do I need to find?** What block comes next.
Step 2 **Plan**	**How will I find the block that comes next?** I will __look for a pattern__.
Step 3 **Solve**	**Find a pattern.** 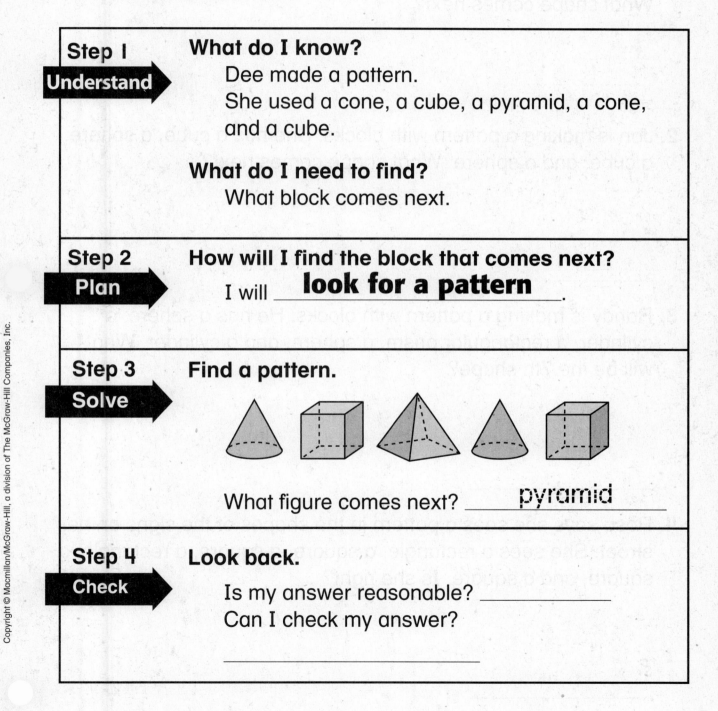 What figure comes next? __pyramid__
Step 4 **Check**	**Look back.** Is my answer reasonable? _____ Can I check my answer? _____

Name _____

Reteach (2)

Problem-Solving Strategy: Look for a Pattern

Find a pattern to solve. Write your answer.

1. Dave is making a pattern with blocks. He has .
   What shape comes next?

   _____

2. Jan is making a pattern with blocks. She has a cube, a sphere, a cube, and a sphere. What shape comes next?

   _____

3. Randy is making a pattern with blocks. He has a sphere, a cylinder, a rectangular prism, a sphere, and a cylinder. What will be the 7th shape?

   _____

4. Rosa says she sees a pattern in the shapes of the signs on her street. She sees a rectangle, a square, a square, a rectangle, a square, and a square. Is she right?

   _____

Name _____

Skills Practice

Problem-Solving Strategy: Look for a Pattern

Find a pattern to solve. Write your answer.

1. Josh is drawing figures.

   He draws .

   Is he drawing a pattern? _____

2. Leo sees this pattern on a poster.

   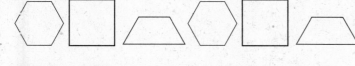

   What three figures come next?

   _____ _____ _____

3. Martha is coloring a row of circles. She colors them red, blue, blue, red, blue, and blue. Is there a pattern? _____ Write the pattern. _____

4. One elephant has one trunk, two ears, and four legs. Two elephants have eight legs. How many legs do five elephants have? _____ legs

5. For one week, Rob and Katie worked for a neighbor. Rob earned $3 a day and Katie earned $4 each day. How much money did they have at the end of seven days?

   _____

Name _____

Reteach

Sides and Vertices

4 vertices ———→ ←— 4 sides

Write how many sides and vertices.

Figure	Sides	Vertices
1. 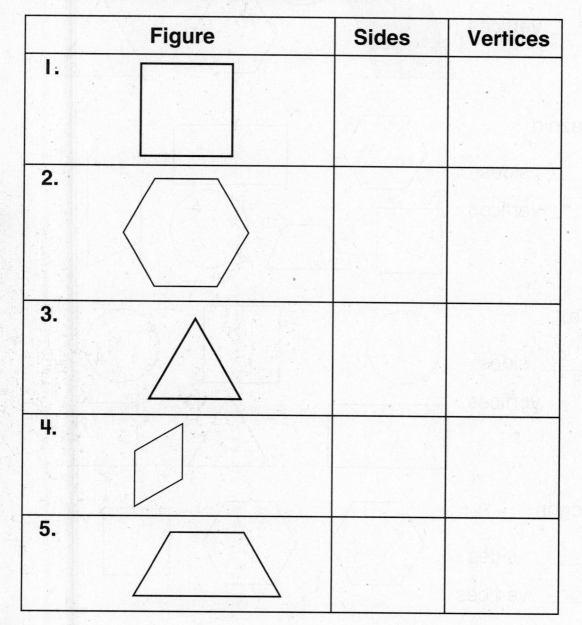		
2.		
3.		
4.		
5.		

Name _____

Skills Practice

Sides and Vertices

Read the name of the figure. Color it. Tell how many sides and vertices it has.

1. parallelogram

    __4__ sides

    __4__ vertices

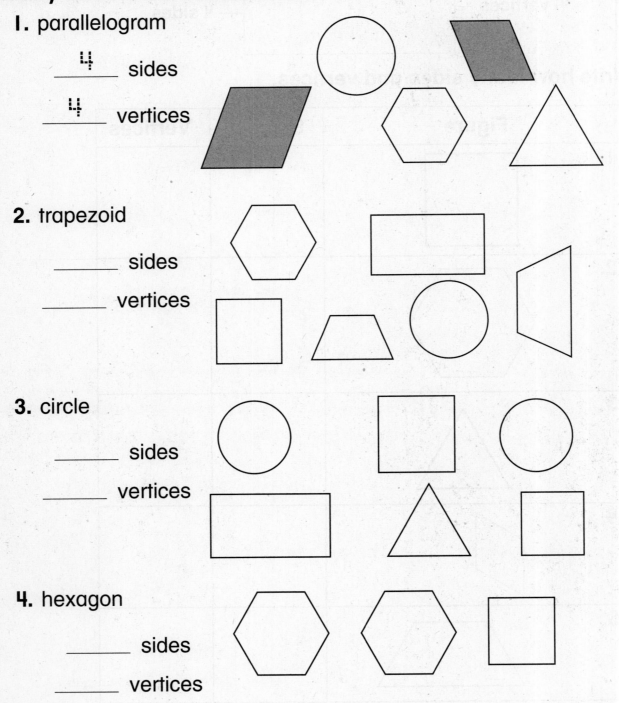

2. trapezoid

    _____ sides

    _____ vertices

3. circle

    _____ sides

    _____ vertices

4. hexagon

    _____ sides

    _____ vertices

222

Name _____

Reteach

Compare Figures

You can compare plane and solid figures by noting how they are alike and different.

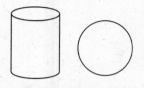

These two figures are alike because both faces of the cylinder are circles.

How are the following figures alike and different?

1.   Alike _____   Different _____

_____   _____

2.   Alike _____   Different _____

_____   _____

3.   Alike _____   Different _____

_____   _____

4.   Alike _____   Different _____

_____   _____

Copyright © Macmillan/McGraw-Hill, a division of The McGraw-Hill Companies, Inc.

Name _____

Skills Practice

Compare Figures

Look at the plane figure in each problem. Circle the solid figure that is like the plane figure.

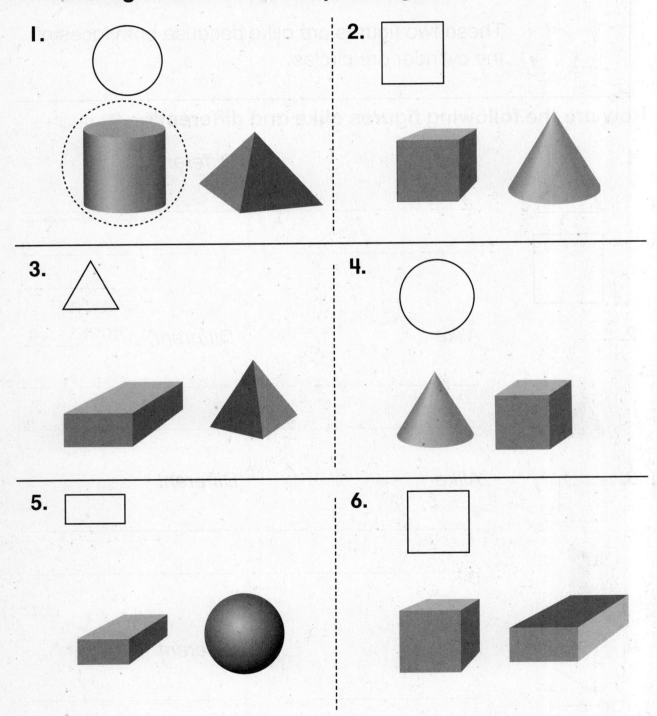

1.

2.

3.

4.

5.

6.

Name ____________________

11-7

Reteach

Make New Figures

Use 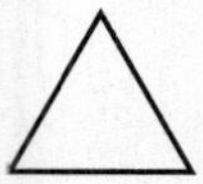 and to make new figures.

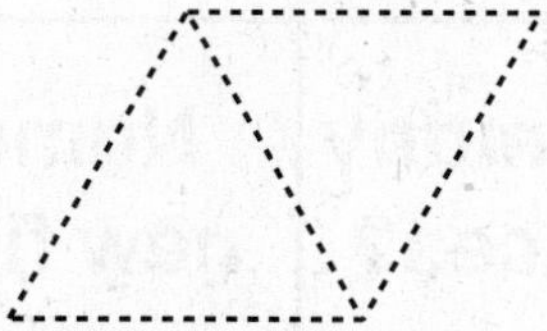

2 triangles can make a parallelogram.
4 sides 4 vertices

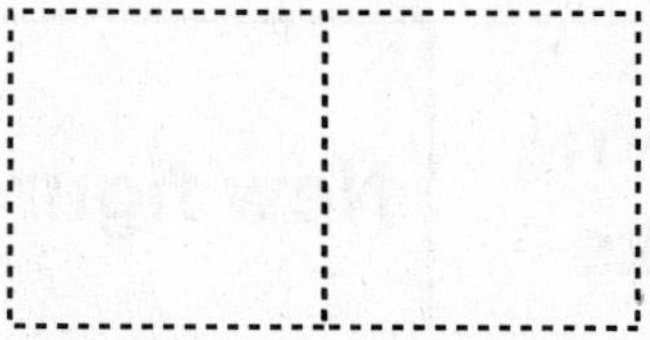

A rectangle can make 2 squares.

---

1. Make a trapezoid using 3 triangles.

Draw the new figure.	How many sides?	How many vertices?

2. Use a hexagon to make new figures.

Draw the new figures.	How many figures?

Name ______________________

11-7 Skills Practice

Make New Figures

Use pattern blocks to make new figures. Complete the chart.

Pattern Blocks	New figure	How many sides?	How many vertices?	Name of new figure
1. 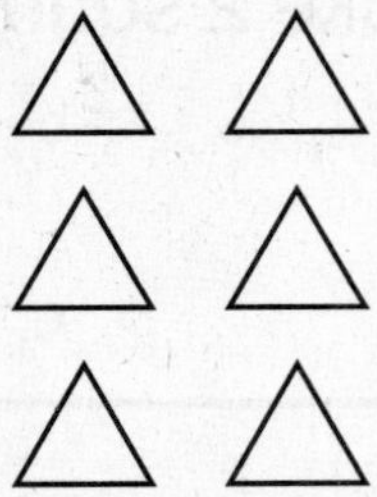		____	____	
2. 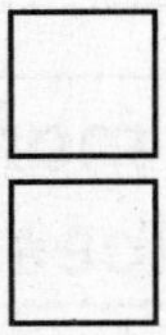		____	____	
3. 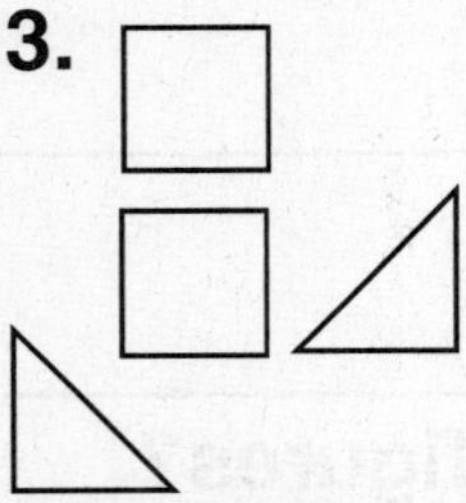		____	____	

Solve. Use pattern blocks to help.

4. Take a hexagon apart. What figures did you get?

____

5. Take a rectangle apart. What figures did you get?

____

Name _____

Reteach (1)

Problem-Solving Investigation: Choose a Strategy

Mia has a block. It is a two-dimensional figure.
It has 6 sides. Each side is the same length.
Which block does Mia have?

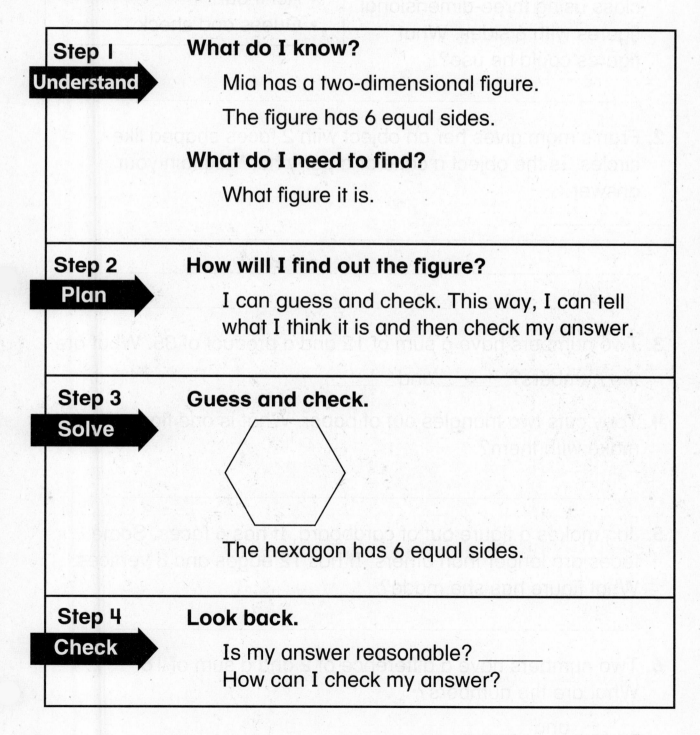

Step 1
Understand

What do I know?

Mia has a two-dimensional figure.

The figure has 6 equal sides.

What do I need to find?

What figure it is.

Step 2
Plan

How will I find out the figure?

I can guess and check. This way, I can tell what I think it is and then check my answer.

Step 3
Solve

Guess and check.

The hexagon has 6 equal sides.

Step 4
Check

Look back.

Is my answer reasonable? _____
How can I check my answer?

Name _____

Reteach (2)

Problem-Solving Investigation: Choose a Strategy

Choose a strategy. Solve.

Problem-Solving Strategies
• Draw a picture
• Act it out
• Guess and check

1. Lau has to design a robot for class using three-dimensional figures with 6 sides. What figures could he use?

_____

2. Fran's mom gives her an object with 2 faces shaped like circles. Is the object a cake or a party hat? Explain your answer.

_____

_____

_____

3. Two numbers have a sum of 12 and a product of 35. What are the numbers? _____ and _____

4. Toby cuts two triangles out of paper. What is one figure he can make with them?

_____

5. Jan makes a figure out of cardboard. It has 6 faces. Some faces are longer than others. It has 12 edges and 8 vertices. What figure has she made?

_____

6. Two numbers have a difference of 2 and a sum of 16. What are the numbers?

_____ and _____

Name _____

Skills Practice

Problem-Solving Investigation: Choose a Strategy

Choose a strategy. Solve.

Problem-Solving Strategies
- Draw a picture
- Act it out
- Guess and check

1. You have 5 coins that total 72¢. What coins do you have?

   _____

   _____

2. Jeff says he wants to draw a cube. How many faces and vertices will he have to draw?

   _____ faces and _____ vertices

3. Mr. Green told his class to draw a pattern using 3 figures.

   Meg made this pattern: ★ ☐ ◯

   Is there a pattern? _____
   Draw a pattern with Meg's figures.

4. Two numbers have a difference of three and a product of 40. What are the numbers?

   _____ and _____

5. I have two faces. I also have no edges or vertices. What figure am I?

   _____

11-9

Reteach

Locate Points on a Number Line

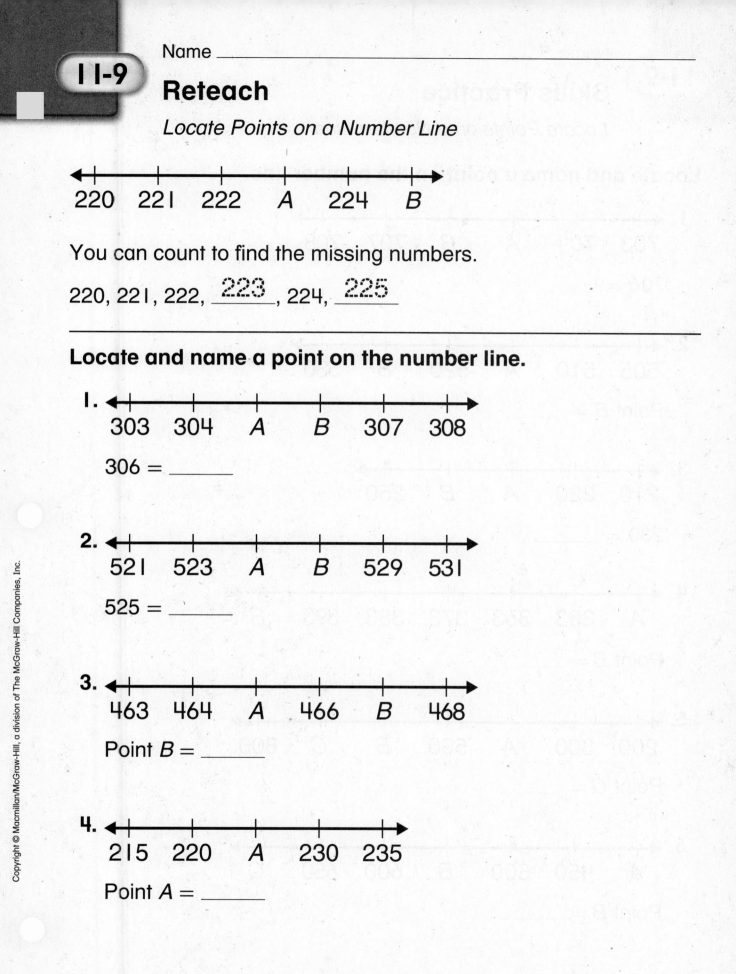

220 221 222 *A* 224 *B*

You can count to find the missing numbers.

220, 221, 222, _223_ , 224, _225_

Locate and name a point on the number line.

1.

303 304 *A* *B* 307 308

306 = _____

2.

521 523 *A* *B* 529 531

525 = _____

3.

463 464 *A* 466 *B* 468

Point *B* = _____

4.

215 220 *A* 230 235

Point *A* = _____

11-9

Skills Practice

Locate Points on a Number Line

Locate and name a point on the number line.

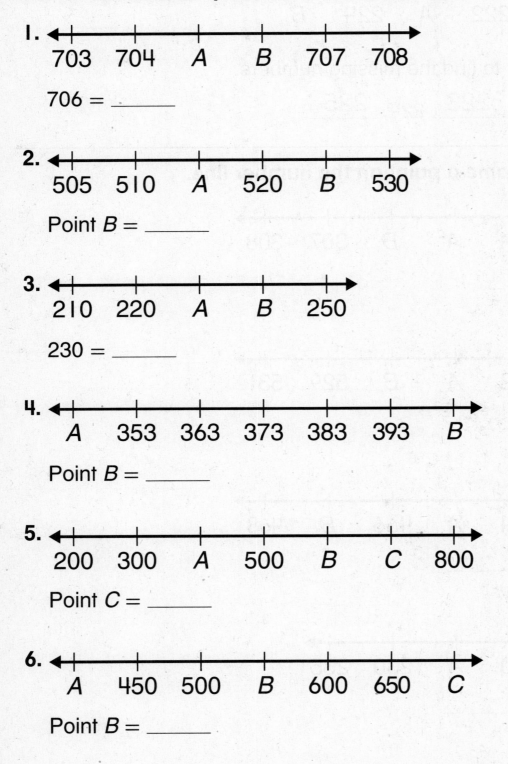

1. 703 704 A B 707 708

706 = _____

2. 505 510 A 520 B 530

Point B = _____

3. 210 220 A B 250

230 = _____

4. A 353 363 373 383 393 B

Point B = _____

5. 200 300 A 500 B C 800

Point C = _____

6. A 450 500 B 600 650 C

Point B = _____

Name _____

Reteach

Coordinate Graphs

You can use a coordinate graph to find where things are located.

- Always start at 0.
- First count to the right. →
- Then count up. ↑
- To find the slide, go to the right 1 and up 2.

Find each point on your graph.
Circle the object at that point.

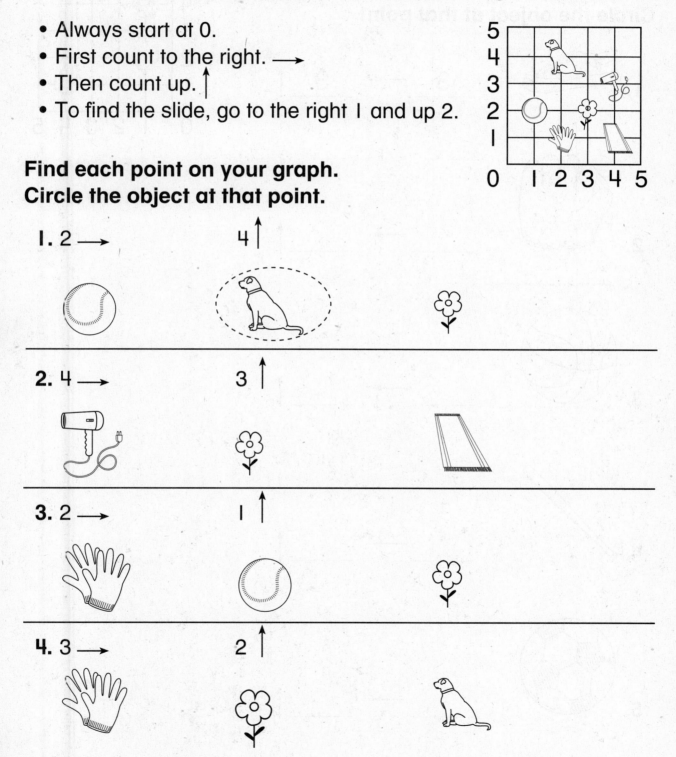

1. 2 →   4 ↑

2. 4 →   3 ↑

3. 2 →   1 ↑

4. 3 →   2 ↑

11-10

Skills Practice

Coordinate Graphs

Find each point on your graph.
Circle the object at that point.

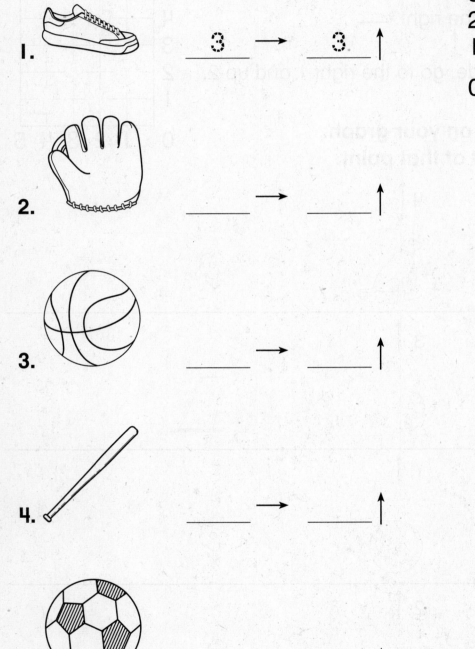

1. _3_ → _3_ ↑

2. ____ → ____ ↑

3. ____ → ____ ↑

4. ____ → ____ ↑

5. ____ → ____ ↑

Reteach

Nonstandard Units

Different units make different measurements.
A 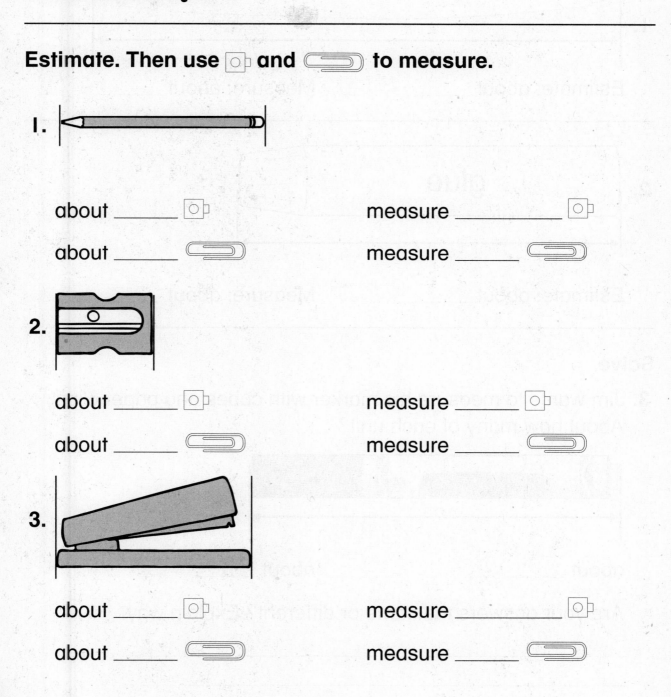 will give a different measurement than a
for the same object.

Estimate. Then use ⬜ and ⬤ to measure.

1.

about _____ ⬜   measure _____ ⬜

about _____ ⬤   measure _____ ⬤

2.

about _____ ⬜   measure _____ ⬜

about _____ ⬤   measure _____ ⬤

3.

about _____ ⬜   measure _____ ⬜

about _____ ⬤   measure _____ ⬤

12-1

Skills Practice

Nonstandard Units

Find the object. Estimate. Then use 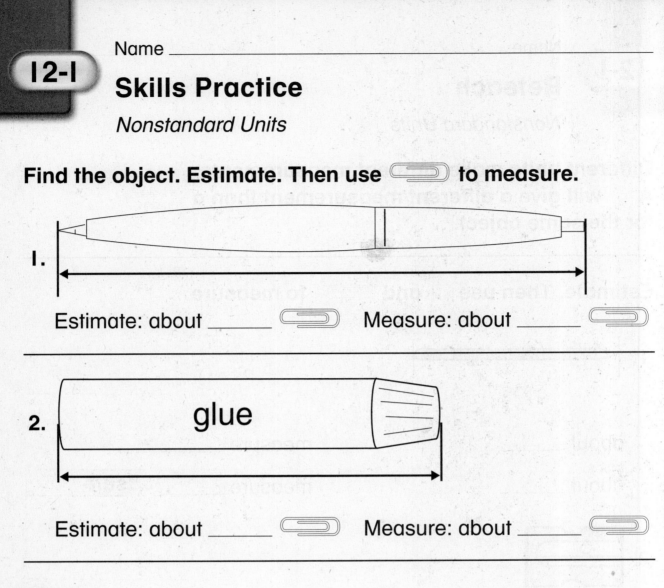 **to measure.**

1.

Estimate: about _____ ⬭   Measure: about _____ ⬭

2.

glue

Estimate: about _____ ⬭   Measure: about _____ ⬭

Solve.

3. Jim wants to measure his marker with cubes and paper clips.
About how many of each unit?

about _____ ⬜   about _____ ⬭

Are your answers the same or different? Explain why.

_____

_____

Name _____

Reteach

Measure Inches Using Models

Use an inch ruler to measure length.

Line up the zero end of the ruler with one end of the pencil. Read the number at the other end of the pencil.

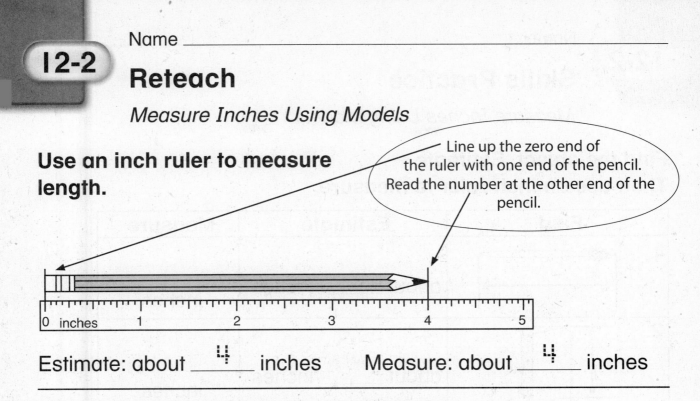

Estimate: about ___4___ inches   Measure: about ___4___ inches

---

Estimate the length of each picture below.
Then use an inch ruler to measure.

Picture	Estimate	Measure
1. blue crayon	about _____ inches	about _____ inches
2. paper clip	about _____ inches	about _____ inches
3. eraser	about _____ inches	about _____ inches
4. chalk	about _____ inches	about _____ inches
5. stapler	about _____ inches	about _____ inches

Name _____

Skills Practice

Measure Inches Using Models

Find the object. Estimate.
Then use an inch ruler to measure.

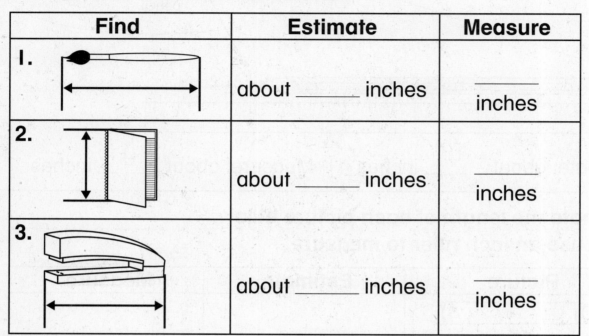

Find	Estimate	Measure
1.	about _____ inches	_____ inches
2.	about _____ inches	_____ inches
3.	about _____ inches	_____ inches

Solve.

4. Ali makes a row of 75¢ in quarters. Each quarter is about one inch long. About how long is Ali's row of quarters? Tell how you know. The row is about _____ inches long.

_____

_____

5. Lu measured one ⬚⬚⬚⬚⬚⬚. It was about 4 inches. She put 3 ⬚⬚⬚⬚⬚⬚ end to end. About how long was the line of three ⬚⬚⬚⬚⬚⬚? Tell how you know.

The line is about _____ inches long.

_____

12-3

Reteach (1)

Problem-Solving Strategy: Guess and Check

Beth wants to glue this leaf to a card.
The card is 3 inches long.
Will the leaf fit?

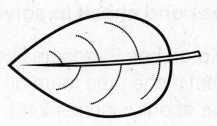

Step 1 **Understand** ▶	**What do I know?** The card is 3 inches long. **What do I need to find?** How long the leaf is.
Step 2 **Plan** ▶	**How will I find the length of the leaf?** I will show 3 inches with three 1 inch ⬭. I will guess by comparing the leaf to the ⬭. Then I will use an inch ruler to check.
Step 3 **Solve** ▶	**Guess and check.** Guess: The leaf is about 1 ⬭ less than the card. I guess that the leaf is ___2___ inches long. Check: The leaf is ___2___ inches long.
Step 4 **Check** ▶	**Look back.** Was my guess close? _____ Did I answer the question? _____

Name _____

Reteach (2)

Problem-Solving Strategy: Guess and Check

Guess and check to solve.

1. Karen has 4 erasers like this one. She says that if she puts them all in a row, the row will be about 6 inches long. Is she correct? _____

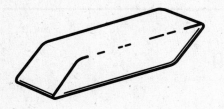

Length of 1 eraser:

Guess: _____   Check: _____ inches

Length of 4 erasers:

Guess: _____   Check: _____ inches

2. Marco's pencil is 6 inches long. Is this feather longer or shorter than Marco's pencil? _____

3. Ben has 10 paper clips. He says that if he puts them all in a row, the row will be about 10 inches long. Is he correct? _____

Length of 1 paper clip:

Guess: _____   Check: _____ inches

Length of 10 paper clips:

Guess: _____   Check: _____ inches

Name _____

Skills Practice

Problem-Solving Strategy: Guess and Check

Guess and check to solve.

1. Luis wants to break this chalk into 2 equal pieces. He wants each piece to be 2 inches long.

   Is this possible? _____

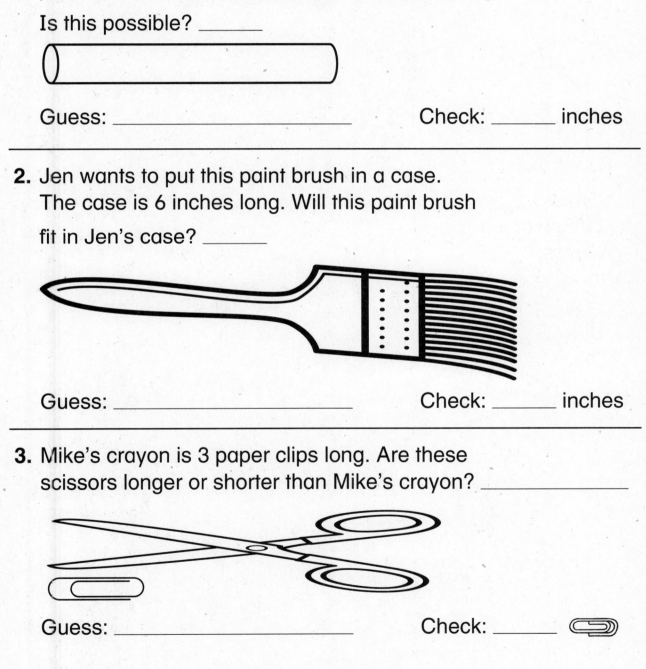

   Guess: _____   Check: _____ inches

---

2. Jen wants to put this paint brush in a case. The case is 6 inches long. Will this paint brush

   fit in Jen's case? _____

   Guess: _____   Check: _____ inches

---

3. Mike's crayon is 3 paper clips long. Are these scissors longer or shorter than Mike's crayon? _____

   Guess: _____   Check: _____

Name _____

Reteach

Use an Inch Ruler

You can measure with inches. Use an inch ruler to measure the length or height of objects.

About how tall is the chair?
Circle the better estimate.

about 6 inches

about 24 inches

Think of the real object. Then circle the better estimate.

1.

   about 5 inches

   about 2 feet

2.

   about 24 inches

   about 7 inches

3. 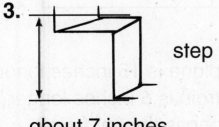 step

   about 7 inches

   about 14 inches

4.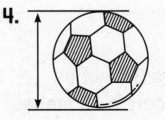

   about 9 inches

   about 18 inches

Name _____

Skills Practice

Use an Inch Ruler

**Find the object. Use inches.
Estimate. Measure each object in the unit shown.**

Find	Estimate	Measure
1.	_____ inch	_____ inch
2.	_____ inches	_____ inches
3.	_____ inches	_____ inches
4.	_____ inches	_____ inches

Solve.

5. Lita's scarf is 36 inches long. Jill's scarf is 12 inches shorter. How long is Jill's scarf?

_____ inches long

6. A toy plane is 15 inches long. A toy train is 6 inches longer. How long is the toy train?

_____ inches long

Reteach

Measure Centimeters Using Models

Use the centimeter ruler to measure.

Line up the zero end of the ruler with one end of the crayon. Read the number at the other end of the crayon.

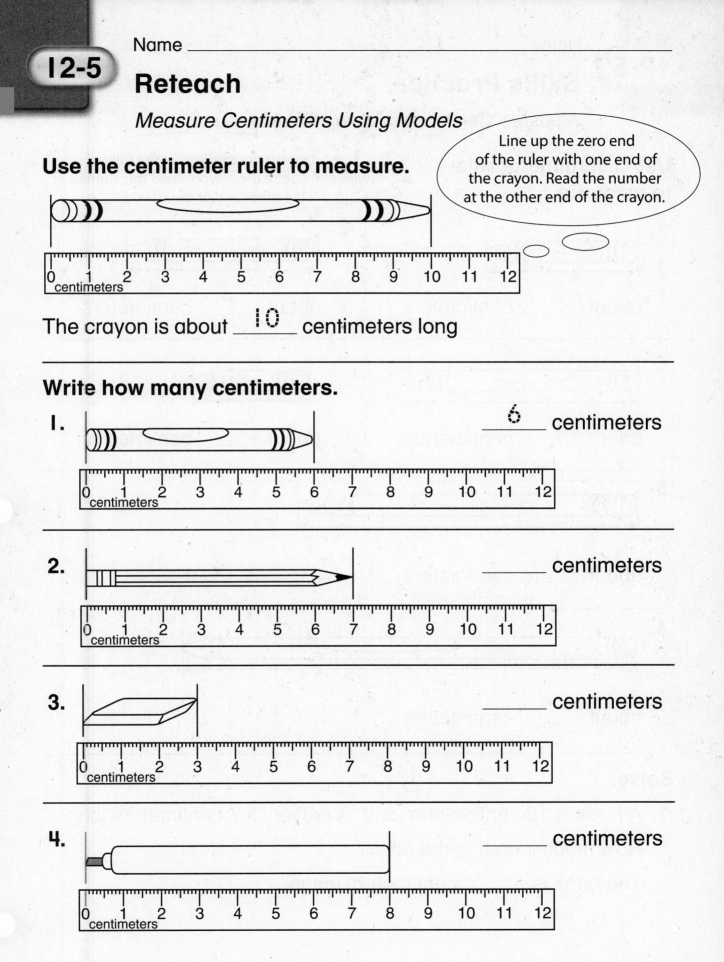

The crayon is about ___10___ centimeters long

___

Write how many centimeters.

I. ___6___ centimeters

2. _____ centimeters

3. _____ centimeters

4. _____ centimeters

12-5

Skills Practice

Measure Centimeters Using Models

Use a centimeter ruler to measure.

Line up the zero end of the ruler with one end of the crayon. Read the number at the other end of the crayon.

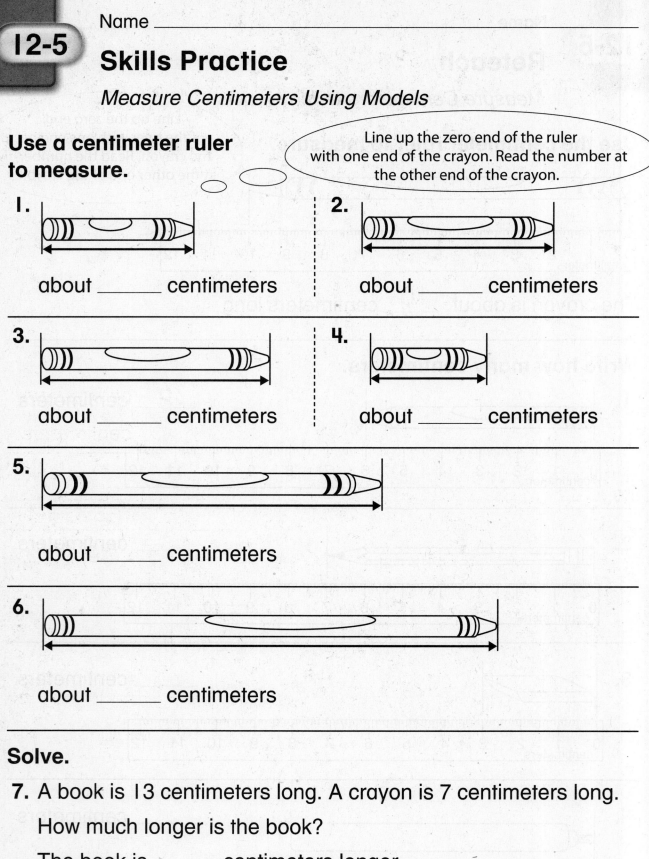

1.

about _____ centimeters

2.

about _____ centimeters

3.

about _____ centimeters

4.

about _____ centimeters

5.

about _____ centimeters

6.

about _____ centimeters

Solve.

7. A book is 13 centimeters long. A crayon is 7 centimeters long.

How much longer is the book?

The book is _____ centimeters longer.

Reteach

Use a Centimeter Ruler

You can measure with centimeters. Use a centimeter ruler to measure the length or height of objects.

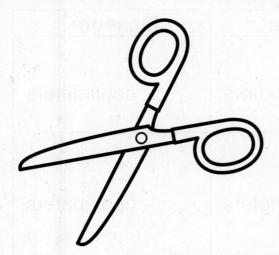

Estimate: about _____ centimeters

Measure: about _____ centimeters

Estimate. Find an object for each length.

Estimate	Object	Measure
1. about 10 centimeters	_____ _____	_____ centimeters
2. about 20 centimeters	_____ _____	_____ centimeters
3. about 30 centimeters	_____ _____	_____ centimeters
4. about 40 centimeters	_____ _____	_____ centimeters

12-6

Skills Practice

Use a Centimeter Ruler

Find the object. Estimate. Measure each object in centimeters.

Find	Estimate	Measure
1.	_____ centimeters	_____ centimeters
2.	_____ centimeters	_____ centimeters
3.	_____ centimeters	_____ centimeters
4.	_____ centimeters	_____ centimeters

5. Name three things in your classroom that are longer than 25 centimeters but shorter than 50 centimeters. Use a centimeter ruler to measure them.

_____

6. Name two things in your classroom that are longer than 50 centimeters. Use a centimeter ruler to measure them.

_____

Reteach (1)

Problem-Solving Investigation: Choose a Strategy

Miguel has $4 saved in his piggy bank.
His sister Maya has $3 saved.
If they put their money together,
how much would they have?

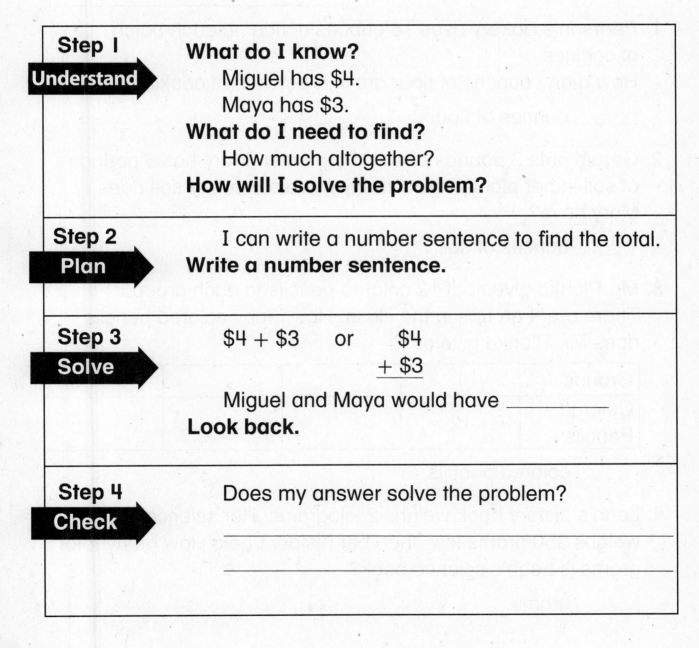

Step 1 **Understand** ▶	**What do I know?** Miguel has $4. Maya has $3. **What do I need to find?** How much altogether? **How will I solve the problem?**
Step 2 **Plan** ▶	I can write a number sentence to find the total. **Write a number sentence.**
Step 3 **Solve** ▶	$4 + $3 or $4 + $3 Miguel and Maya would have _____ **Look back.**
Step 4 **Check** ▶	Does my answer solve the problem? _____ _____

Name _____

Reteach (2)

Problem-Solving Investigation: Choose a Strategy

Choose a strategy. Solve.

Problem-Solving Strategies
• Write a number sentence
• Make a table
• Draw a picture

1. Pearson's Bakery uses 16 ounces of flour in each batch of cookies.
   How many ounces of flour are in 4 batches of cookies?

   _____ ounces of flour

2. Gerald puts 3 pounds of soil in a planter. Mary has 5 pounds of soil in her planter. How many more ounces of soil does Mary have?

   _____ ounces of soil

3. Mr. Plonka gives out 12 colored pencils to each group. There are 4 groups in the class. How many colored pencils does Mr. Plonka give out?

Groups	1			
Colored Pencils	12			

   _____ colored pencils

4. Leah's history book weighs 2 kilograms. Her science book weighs 250 grams less than her history book. How many total grams is Leah's science book?

   _____ grams

13-8

Skills Practice

Problem-Solving Investigation: Choose a Strategy

Choose a strategy. Solve.

Problem-Solving Strategies
• Write a number sentence
• Make a table
• Draw a picture

1. Gina's school had a bakesale. They sold 14 gallons of water and 19 gallons of punch. How many gallons were sold in all?

   _____ gallons

2. Jay, May and Ray stand in line. Ray is behind May. May is behind Jay. Who is in front?

   _____

3. Brown School's second-grade class has a picnic. Mrs. Lee pours 1 cup of juice for each student. If there are 53 second-graders, how many gallons of juice does Mrs. Lee need?

Cups	16			
Gallons	1			

   _____ gallons

4. Micah's library book weighs 4 kilograms. Grace's book weighs 400 grams less than Micah's book. How many total grams is Grace's book?

   _____ grams

Name _____

Reteach

Add Hundreds

Using a model can help add hundreds.

200   +   300   =   ?

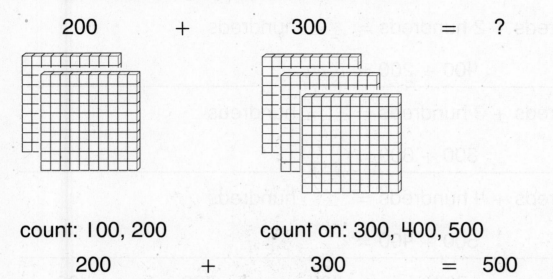

count: 100, 200   count on: 300, 400, 500

200   +   300   =   500

Use hundred cubes to model each problem. Write your answer.

1.   100   +   200   = _____

---

2. $100 + 300 =$ _____   3. $200 + 200 =$ _____

4. $100 + 100 =$ _____   5. $200 + 300 =$ _____

6. $200 + 100 =$ _____   7. $400 + 100 =$ _____

Name _____

Skills Practice

Add Hundreds

Add.

1. 4 hundreds + 2 hundreds = _____ hundreds

   $$400 + 200 = \text{\_\_\_\_}$$

2. 3 hundreds + 3 hundreds = _____ hundreds

   $$300 + 300 = \text{\_\_\_\_}$$

3. 5 hundreds + 4 hundreds = _____ hundreds

   $$500 + 400 = \text{\_\_\_\_}$$

4.
200	500	400	700	400
+ 100	+ 200	+ 300	+ 100	+ 200

Solve.

5. Kal has 400 pennies. His sister also has 400 pennies. How many pennies do they have in all?

   _____ hundreds + _____ hundreds = _____ hundreds

   $$400 + 400 = \text{\_\_\_\_ pennies}$$

6. Joy has 300 stickers. Juan has 500 stickers. How many total stickers are there? Write a number sentence to solve.

   _____ hundreds + _____ hundreds = _____ hundreds

   _____ + _____ = _____ stickers

Name _____

Reteach

Regroup Ones

You can use base-ten blocks to model regrouping.

| Find 247 + 136. |

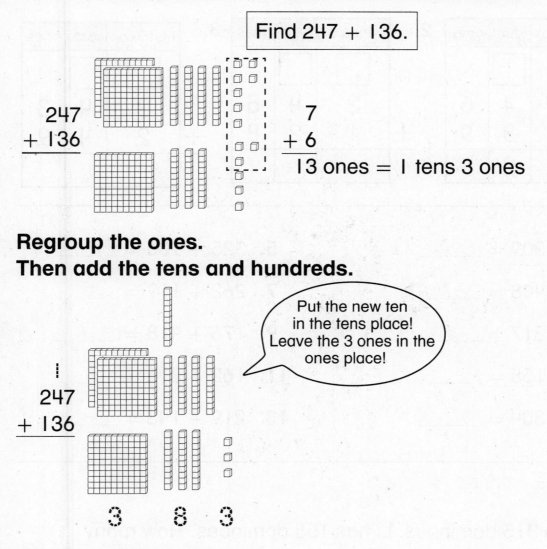

247
+ 136

7
+ 6
____
13 ones = 1 tens 3 ones

Regroup the ones.
Then add the tens and hundreds.

247
+ 136

Put the new ten
in the tens place!
Leave the 3 ones in the
ones place!

3   8   3

So, 247 + 136 = 383

Use base-ten blocks to model each problem.
Regroup blocks to solve.

1. 129 + 203 = _____

2. 262 + 119 = _____

3. 288 + 306 = _____

4. 469 + 228 = _____

277

14-2

Skills Practice

Regroup Ones

Use models and WorkMat 7. Add.

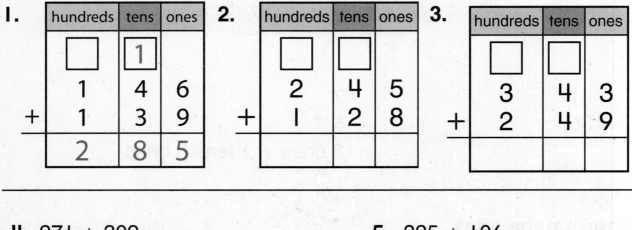

1.

hundreds	tens	ones
□	1	
1	4	6
+ 1	3	9
2	8	5

2.

hundreds	tens	ones
□	□	
2	4	5
+ 1	2	8

3.

hundreds	tens	ones
□	□	
3	4	3
+ 2	4	9

4. $271 + 309 =$ _____

5. $325 + 106 =$ _____

6. $183 + 408 =$ _____

7. $262 + 119 =$ _____

8. $364 + 317 =$ _____

9. $176 + 418 =$ _____

10. $237 + 155 =$ _____

11. $162 + 318 =$ _____

12. $308 + 304 =$ _____

13. $219 + 143 =$ _____

Solve.

14. Ira has 315 dominoes. Li has 158 dominoes. How many dominoes in all?

_____ dominoes

15. Jose has 224 marbles. Bess has 357 marbles. How many total marbles?

_____ marbles

Name _____

Reteach

Regroup Tens

**If there are 10 or more tens, you need to regroup.
A model can help regroup tens.**

Find 370 + 290. Draw your models.

Use ⬜ for hundreds and | for tens.

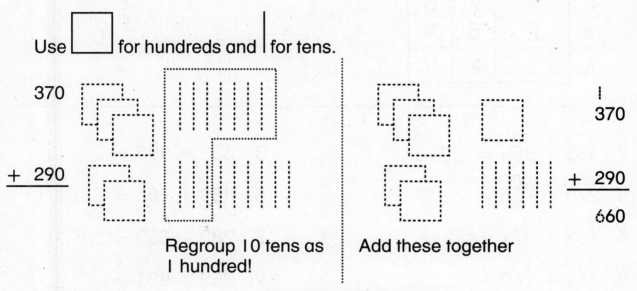

Regroup 10 tens as
1 hundred!

Add these together

So, 370 + 290 = 660

_____

Draw models to help you add.

1. 290 + 350 = _____

Show your work here.

2. 120 + 280 = _____

Name _____

Skills Practice

Regroup Tens

Use models and WorkMat 7. Add.

1.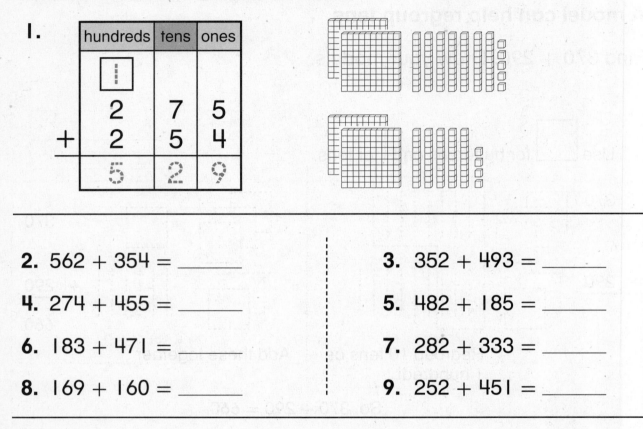

hundreds	tens	ones
1		
2	7	5
+ 2	5	4
5	2	9

2. 562 + 354 = _____

3. 352 + 493 = _____

4. 274 + 455 = _____

5. 482 + 185 = _____

6. 183 + 471 = _____

7. 282 + 333 = _____

8. 169 + 160 = _____

9. 252 + 451 = _____

Solve.

10. Kay has 429 rocks in her collection. She finds 390 more. How many rocks does Kay have?

   _____

11. Luis has 543 baseball cards. His sister has 362. How many cards do they have in all?

   _____

Name _____

Reteach (1)

Problem-Solving Strategy: Make a Table

Maya and Tom want to take a class.
Maya has soccer practice until 4:00.
Tom has a piano lesson at 6:00.
Which class can they take?

World Cooking Classes		
Class	Time Class Starts	Time Class Ends
African Treats	2:00	3:00
French Food	3:00	4:30
Chinese Cooking	4:30	5:00
Mexican Dinners	5:00	7:00

Step 1
Understand

What do I know?

Maya is busy until 4:00.
Tom is busy after 6:00.

What do I need to find?

Which cooking class they both can take.

Step 2
Plan

How will I find out which class they both can take?

I will find a class that begins after 4:00 for Maya and ends before 6:00 for Tom.

Step 3
Solve

Write down information from the table.

Maya can make the 4:30 and 5:00 classes.

Tom cannot make the 5:00 class.

They can both take _____.

Step 4
Check

Look back.

How did the table help me to answer the question? _____

Name _____

Reteach (2)

Problem-Solving Strategy: Make a Table

Use the tables to solve.

1. A storyteller is coming to the library on Saturday. Jack has a swimming lesson until 12:00. Flora wants to hear a story that is an hour long. Which story should Jack and Flora listen to?

Story	Time Story Starts	Time Story Ends
Wolf and the Drum	11:00	12:00
Old Man Winter	12:30	1:00
Tina Races the Tiger	1:00	2:00
Rabbit's New Vest	2:00	2:30

2. Andre has $4. Then, he buys a gift for his mom.

a bunch of daisies	$3
beaded ring	$2
toy cat	$1

He has some money left, so he buys the toy cat for his sister. Now Andre has $1. What did he buy for his mom?

_____

3. Ms. Ling's class is going to the science museum. She made a list of the activities for the day.

Museum Trip	
see space models	9:30–10:30
see movie: On the Moon	10:30–12:00
eat lunch	12:00–1:00
See dinosaur bones	1:00–2:00

How long is the movie? _____

Name _____

Skills Practice

Problem-Solving Strategy: Make a Table

Use the table to answer the questions.

Flights to Seattle from Minneapolis:

Flight Number	Leaves	Arrives
206	7:10	1:20
305	9:30	4:00
491	12:50	6:50
511	6:05	12:15

1. Paul leaves for Seattle on Flight 305. Tom leaves on Flight 206. How long will Tom arrive before Paul arrives?

_____

2. Jane is taking Flight 491 to Seattle. The plane leaves an hour late. What time will the plane arrive in Seattle? _____

3. Which flight is longer than the others? _____

Complete the table to solve.

4. There are 10 people in each raft. How many people are in 5 rafts?

Rafts	1				
People	10				

Name _____

Reteach

Estimate Sums

You can estimate to find an answer that is close to the exact answer.

There are 517 people in Cold Creek. There are 281 people in Old Town. About how many people live in the two towns?

Step 1

Look at the tens. Round each addend to the nearest **hundred**.

517 rounds to → 500
+ 281 rounds to → + 300

Step 2

Add the new addends to find the estimated sum.

500
+ 300
800

The number of people in the two towns is about _____.

Round each number to the nearest *hundred*. Estimate each sum.

1. 489 →
    + 311 → +

2. 466 →
    + 195 → +

Round each number to the nearest *ten*. Estimate each sum.

3. 606 →
    + 247 → +

4. 307 →
    + 258 → +

Name _____

Skills Practice

Estimate Sums

Round each number to the nearest *ten*.
Estimate the sum.

1.   302 →
       + 287 → + _____

2.   686 →
       + 174 → + _____

3.   365 →
       + 209 → + _____

4.   405 →
       + 325 → + _____

Round each number to the nearest *hundred*.
Estimate the sum.

5.   518 →
       + 169 → + _____

6.   701 →
       + 216 → + _____

7.   176 →
       + 315 → + _____

8.   390 →
       + 412 → + _____

Solve.

9. There are 410 parents and 526 children in the park. Rounding to the nearest hundred, how many people are in the park?

   _____ people

10. Mr. Tan sells 215 apples on Wednesday and 486 apples on Sunday. Rounding to the nearest ten, how many apples does

    Mr. Tan sell? _____ apples

Name _____

Reteach

Subtract Hundreds

Use subtraction facts to subtract hundreds.

Find $600 - 300$.

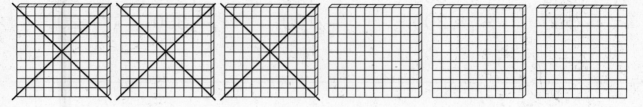

6 hundreds − 3 hundreds = _____ hundreds

$600 - 300 =$ _____

Subtract.

1. 4 hundreds − 1 hundred = _____ hundreds

$400 - 100 =$ _____

---

2. 7 hundreds − 3 hundreds = _____ hundreds

$700 - 300 =$ _____

---

3. 8 hundreds − 5 hundreds = _____ hundreds

$800 - 500 =$ _____

4.

$$\begin{array}{r} 600 \\ -\ 100 \\ \hline \end{array} \qquad \begin{array}{r} 500 \\ -\ 200 \\ \hline \end{array} \qquad \begin{array}{r} 800 \\ -\ 300 \\ \hline \end{array} \qquad \begin{array}{r} 600 \\ -\ 200 \\ \hline \end{array} \qquad \begin{array}{r} 500 \\ -\ 100 \\ \hline \end{array}$$

Name _____

Skills Practice

Subtract Hundreds

Subtract.

1. 300	800	700	600	600
− 100	− 300	− 100	− 300	− 200

2. 400	500	600	800	500
− 100	− 100	− 500	− 100	− 300

3. 500	900	600	700	800
− 200	− 200	− 400	− 400	− 500

Solve.   **Show your work here.**

4. 900 children are in the park.
   700 adults are in the park.
   How many more children
   are there than adults?

   _____ more children

5. 800 people see a movie on
   Friday. 900 people see the
   movie on Saturday. How
   many more people go to the
   movie on Saturday?

   _____ more people

Name _____

Reteach

Regroup Tens

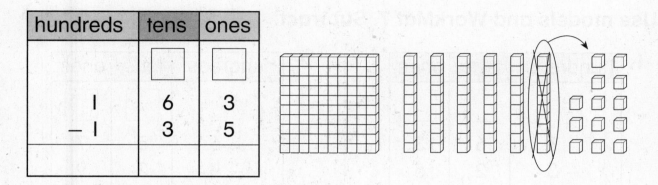

hundreds	tens	ones
	☐	☐
1	6	3
− 1	3	5

Remember: regroup 1 ten as 10 ones.

Use the models to subtract.

1.

hundreds	tens	ones
	☐	☐
4	3	7
− 2	1	8

Use models and WorkMat 7. Subtract.

2. 321 − 13 = _____

3. 549 − 211 = _____

4. 869 − 5 = _____

5. 623 − 415 = _____

6. 460 − 152 = _____

7. 708 − 26 = _____

Name _____

Skills Practice

Regroup Tens

Use models and WorkMat 7. Subtract.

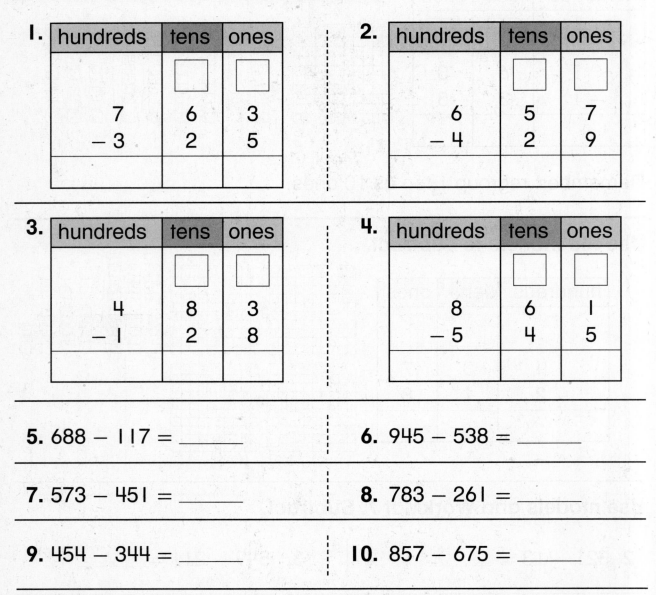

1.

hundreds	tens	ones
	☐	☐
7	6	3
− 3	2	5

2.

hundreds	tens	ones
	☐	☐
6	5	7
− 4	2	9

3.

hundreds	tens	ones
	☐	☐
4	8	3
− 1	2	8

4.

hundreds	tens	ones
	☐	☐
8	6	1
− 5	4	5

5. 688 − 117 = _____

6. 945 − 538 = _____

7. 573 − 451 = _____

8. 783 − 261 = _____

9. 454 − 344 = _____

10. 857 − 675 = _____

Solve.

11. 377 people see a play on Friday night. 495 people see a play on Saturday. How many more people see the play on Saturday?

_____ people

Name _____

Reteach

Regroup Hundreds

Step 1	**Step 2**	**Step 3**
Subtract the ones.	**Subtract the tens.**	**Subtract the**
Write how many ones are left.	Regroup 1 hundred as 10 tens. Write the new number of hundreds and tens in the boxes.	**hundreds.** Write how many hundreds are left.

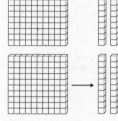

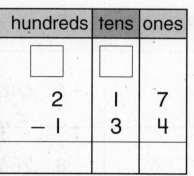

hundreds	tens	ones
☐	☐	
2	1	7
− 1	3	4

hundreds	tens	ones
☐	☐	
2	1	7
− 1	3	4

hundreds	tens	ones
☐	☐	
2	1	7
− 1	3	4

Use models and WorkMat 7. Subtract.

1. $827 - 433 =$ _____

2. $245 - 153 =$ _____

3. $597 - 489 =$ _____

4. $762 - 234 =$ _____

5. $624 - 325 =$ _____

6. $943 - 144 =$ _____

Name _____

Skills Practice

Regroup Hundreds

Use models and WorkMat 7. Subtract.

hundreds	tens	ones
	□	
3	2	8
− 2	7	7

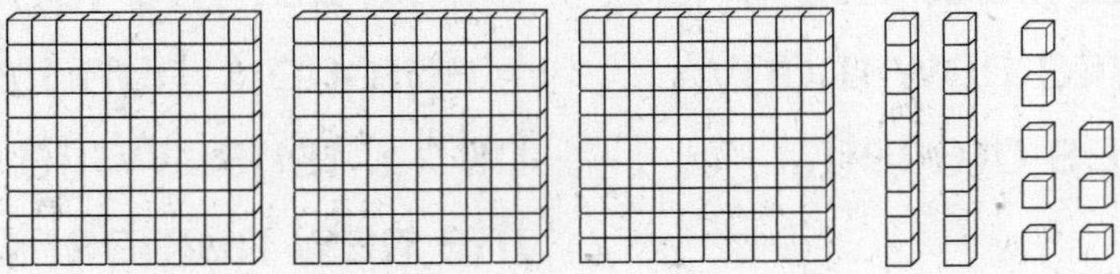

1. $567 − 295 =$ _____

2. $912 − 562 =$ _____

3. $727 − 382 =$ _____

4. $838 − 445 =$ _____

5. $478 − 416 =$ _____

6. $648 − 377 =$ _____

7. $346 − 268 =$ _____

8. $256 − 131 =$ _____

9. $871 − 596 =$ _____

10. $158 − 98 =$ _____

Solve. Show your work.

11. Penny had 347 pumpkins for sale. She sold 255 pumpkins.

How many pumpkins did Penny have left? _____ pumpkins

Name _____

Reteach

Estimate Differences

About how many more miles is it from Chicago to Cleveland than from Chicago to Detroit?

Estimate 315 − 234.

From:	To:	Distance:
Chicago, IL	Cleveland, OH	315 miles
Chicago, IL	Detroit, MI	234 miles

Round to the nearest ten

Round 315 up to 320.
234 is closer to 230 than 240.

$$\begin{array}{r} 315 \\ -\ 234 \end{array} \text{ rounds to } \begin{array}{r} 320 \\ -\ 230 \end{array}$$

The difference in miles is about _____ miles.

Round to the nearest hundred

315 is closer to 300 than 400.
234 is closer to 200 than 300.

$$\begin{array}{r} 315 \\ -\ 234 \end{array} \text{ rounds to } \begin{array}{r} 300 \\ -\ 200 \end{array}$$

The difference in miles is about _____ miles.

		nearest ten		nearest hundred		exact
1.	687 $\longrightarrow$	690 $\longrightarrow$		700		687
	− 279 $\longrightarrow$	− 280 $\longrightarrow$		− 300		− 279
2.	571 $\longrightarrow$	570 $\longrightarrow$		600		571
	− 194 $\longrightarrow$	− 190 $\longrightarrow$		− 200		− 194

Name _____

Skills Practice

Estimate Differences

**Round each number to the nearest *ten*.
Estimate each difference.**

1.
$$255 - 135$$
$$713 - 645$$
$$926 - 406$$
$$841 - 452$$

2.
$$501 - 398$$
$$488 - 216$$
$$377 - 164$$
$$667 - 325$$

3. **Round each number to the nearest *hundred*.
Estimate each difference.**

$$487 - 244$$
$$705 - 280$$
$$376 - 111$$
$$947 - 321$$

Solve

4. Mae's family drives 467 miles on Saturday and 391 miles on Sunday. Rounding to the nearest ten, estimate the difference in miles.

   _____

5. Jake's school has a book sale every year. Last year, the school sold 209 books. They sell 311 books this year. Rounding to the nearest hundred, estimate the difference in books.

   _____

Name _____

Reteach (1)

Problem-Solving Investigation: Choose a Strategy

Mia has 600 marbles. She gives 200 to her friend Nate. Mia gives some to Ray. Mia has 200 marbles left. How many did she give to Ray?

Problem-Solving Strategies

- Find a pattern
- Work backward
- Use logical reasoning

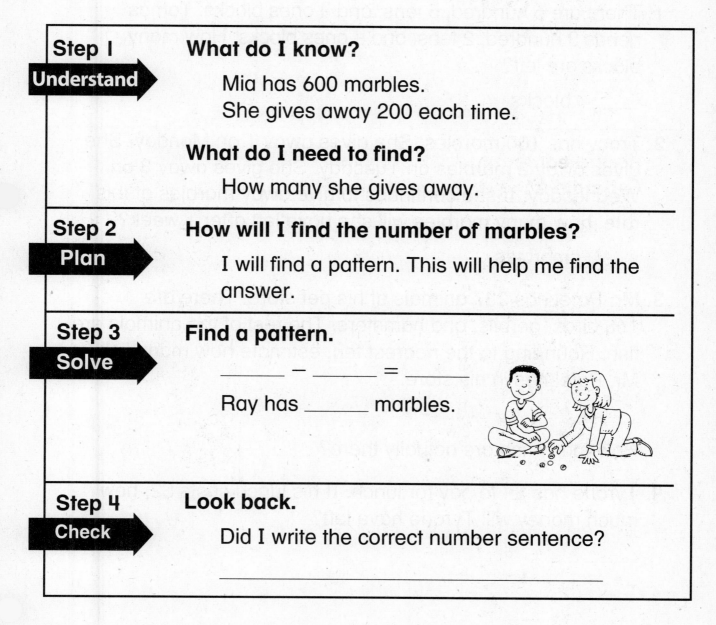

Step 1 Understand

What do I know?

Mia has 600 marbles.
She gives away 200 each time.

What do I need to find?

How many she gives away.

Step 2 Plan

How will I find the number of marbles?

I will find a pattern. This will help me find the answer.

Step 3 Solve

Find a pattern.

_____ − _____ = _____

Ray has _____ marbles.

Step 4 Check

Look back.

Did I write the correct number sentence?

_____

Name _____

Reteach (2)

Problem-Solving Investigation: Choose a Strategy

Choose a strategy to solve.

Problem-Solving Strategies
• Find a pattern
• Work backward
• Use logical reasoning

1. There are 6 hundred, 5 tens, and 4 ones blocks. Tomas needs 3 hundred, 2 tens, and 4 ones blocks. How many blocks are left?

   _____ blocks

2. Tracy has 100 marbles. She gives away 1 on Monday. She gives away 2 marbles on Tuesday. She gives away 3 on Wednesday. If she continues to give away marbles at this rate, how many marbles will she have left after 1 week?

   _____ marbles

3. Mr. Patel has 237 animals at his pet store. There are 168 birds, gerbils, and hamsters. The rest of the animals are fish. Rounding to the nearest ten, estimate how many fish Mr. Patel has in his store.

   _____

   How many fish are actually there? _____

4. Tyrone has $4 to pay for lunch. If his lunch costs $2, how much money will Tyrone have left?

   _____

14-10

Skills Practice

Problem-Solving Investigation: Choose a Strategy

Choose a strategy to solve.

Problem-Solving Strategies
• Find a pattern
• Work backward
• Use logical reasoning

1. Mrs. Dahl has 9 hundred, 7 tens, and 8 ones blocks. Al borrows 2 hundreds, 5 tens, and 5 ones blocks. How many blocks are left?

   _____ blocks

2. Nell and Sam save 620 pennies. They put 372 pennies in a blue can. They put the rest in a red can. How many pennies do they put in the red can?

   _____ pennies

3. Mrs. Robbin's science class plants seeds. On Tuesday 2 seeds sprout. 4 sprout on Wednesday. 6 come up on Thursday. If the pattern continues, how many seeds will have sprouted on Friday in all?

   _____ seeds

4. Josh has some money to buy a present for his dad. He spends $5 on the present. He spends another $1 for a big ribbon. He has $2 left. How much money did Josh start with?

   _____

Name _____

Reteach

Multiplication Stories

You can make models to solve multiplication stories.

There are 3 lunch tables.
3 students sit at each table.
How many students are
there in all?

_____9_____

Cut out the faces. Glue faces to model each multiplication story. Count the faces to solve.

1. There are 2 benches.
3 students sit on each bench.
How many students are there? _____ students

2. There are 4 trees.
2 students climb in each tree.
How many students are there? _____ students

Name _____

Skills Practice

Multiplication Stories

Use counters to model multiplication sentences.
Count to solve.

1. There are 3 bowls.
   4 plums are in each bowl.
   How many plums are there?

   _____ plums

2. There are 2 cartons.
   4 peaches are in each carton.
   How many peaches are there?

   _____ peaches

3. There are 3 sacks.
   2 melons are in each sack.
   How many melons are there?

   _____ melons

4. There are 4 bags.
   3 oranges are in each bag.
   How many oranges are there?

   _____ oranges

15-2

Reteach

Equal Groups

Use ⬤ to keep track of equal groups.

Place a ⬤ on each equal group. Then count to see how many equal groups.

_____ equal groups

_____

Use ⬤ to count equal groups.

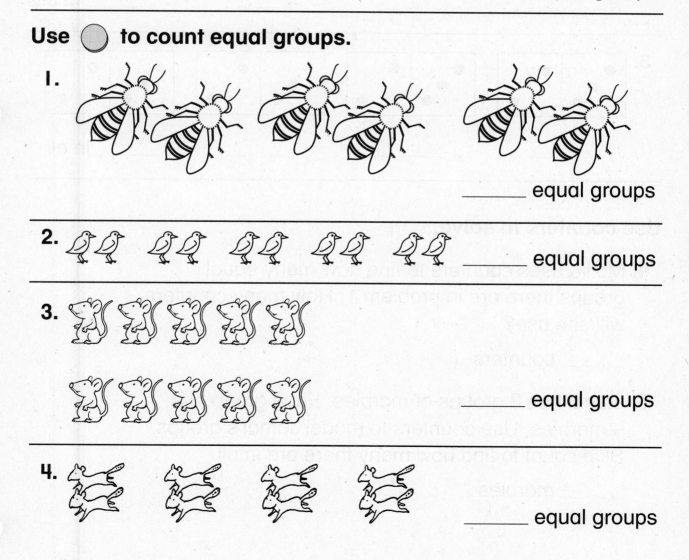

1.

_____ equal groups

2.

_____ equal groups

3.

_____ equal groups

4.

_____ equal groups

Name _____

Skills Practice

Equal Groups

Skip count. Write how many in all.

1.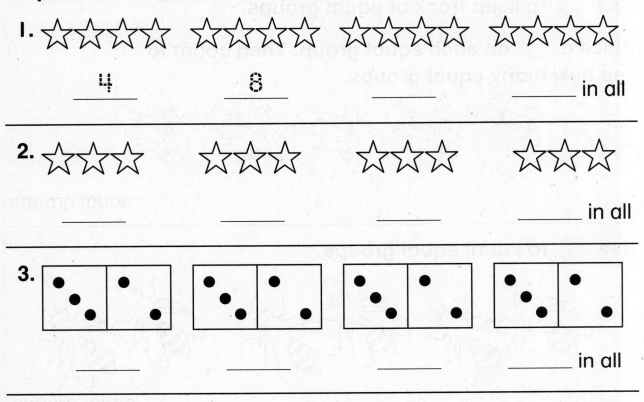

   ___4___   ___8___   _____   _____ in all

2.

   _____   _____   _____   _____ in all

3.

   _____   _____   _____   _____ in all

Use counters to solve.

4. Mollie uses counters to find how many equal
   groups there are in problem 1. How many counters
   will she use?

   _____ counters

5. Jamal has 3 groups of marbles. Each group has
   4 marbles. Use counters to model Jamal's groups.
   Skip count to find how many there are in all.

   _____ marbles

15-3

Reteach (1)

Problem-Solving Strategy: Draw a Picture

Sanders' Orchard sells bags of apples. Each bag has 4 apples. Mary buys 4 bags. How many apples does she buy?

Step 1 **Understand**	**What do I know?** Each bag has 4 apples. Mary buys 4 bags. **What do I need to find out?** How many apples does Mary buy?
Step 2 **Plan**	**How will I find out?** I will draw circles for each of Mary's bags. I will draw 4 apples in each bag.
Step 3 **Solve**	**Draw a picture.** 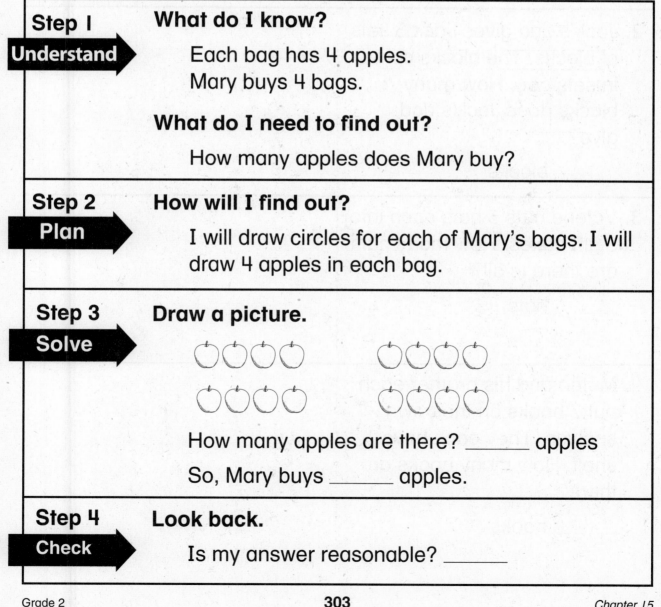 How many apples are there? _____ apples So, Mary buys _____ apples.
Step 4 **Check**	**Look back.** Is my answer reasonable? _____

15-3

Reteach (2)

Problem-Solving Strategy: Draw a Picture

Draw a picture to solve.   **Show your work here.**

1. A.J., Vic, and Maria each
   have a sack of pears. There
   are 4 pears in each sack.
   How many pears do they
   have in all?

   _____ pears

2. Jack's dad gives Jack 3 sets
   of blocks. The blocks come
   in sets of 6. How many
   blocks does Jack's dad
   give?

   _____ blocks

3. Valerie puts 5 hats each into
   3 gift boxes. How many hats
   are there in all?

   _____ hats

4. Mateo and his brother each
   put 7 books on their own
   shelves. They each have 1
   shelf. How many books are
   there?

   _____ books

15-3

Skills Practice

Problem-Solving Strategy: Draw a Picture

Draw a picture to solve. | **Show your work here.**

1. There are 5 moving vans. Each van can hold 4 crates. How many crates can the vans hold, altogether?

_____ crates

2. Leona has 6 boxes. If she puts 4 plates in each box, how many plates boxes will Leona pack?

_____ plates

3. Ivan gives 3 balloons to each of his 4 cousins. How many total balloons does Ivan give?

_____ balloons

4. Ms. Kim gives 3 paint pots to each of her 5 students. How many paint pots does she give in all?

_____ paint pots

Reteach

Repeated Addition

Put a ⬭ on each group. Count the ⬭.

1. 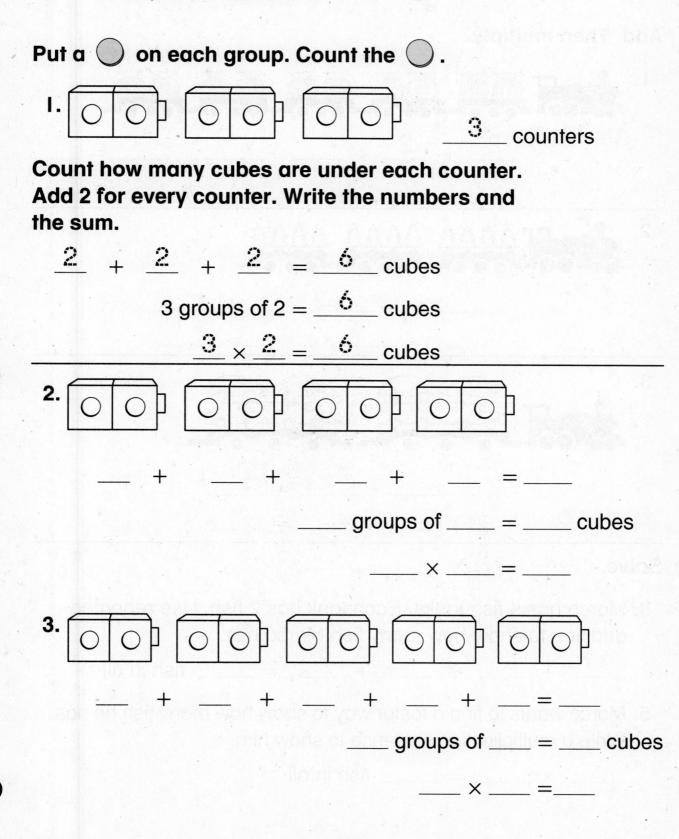 _3_ counters

**Count how many cubes are under each counter.
Add 2 for every counter. Write the numbers and
the sum.**

_2_ + _2_ + _2_ = _6_ cubes

3 groups of 2 = _6_ cubes

_3_ × _2_ = _6_ cubes

2. __ + __ + __ + __ = __

____ groups of ____ = ____ cubes

____ × ____ = ____

3. __ + __ + __ + __ + __ = __

____ groups of ____ = ____ cubes

____ × ____ = ____

Name _____

Skills Practice

Repeated Addition

Add. Then multiply.

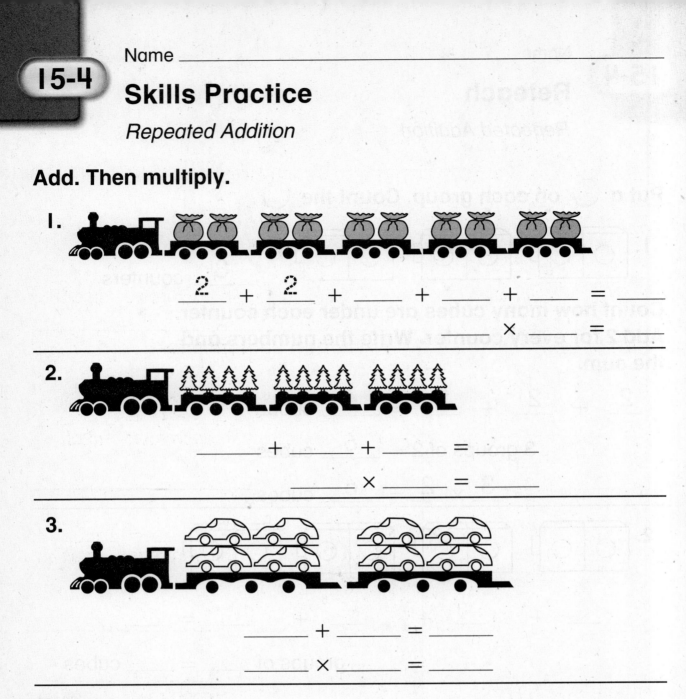

1. ___ + ___ + ___ + ___ + ___ = ___
    2   2

   ___ × ___ = ___

2. ___ + ___ + ___ = ___

   ___ × ___ = ___

3. ___ + ___ = ___

   ___ × ___ = ___

Solve.

4. Marco has 4 fish tanks. Each tank has 2 fish. Use repeated addition to show how many fish Marco has.

   _____ + _____ + _____ + _____ = _____ fish in all

5. Marco wants to find a faster way to show how many fish he has. Write a multiplication sentence to show him.

   _____ × _____ = _____ fish in all

15-5

Reteach

Arrays

Color each row a different color. Count how many rows. Count how many in each row.

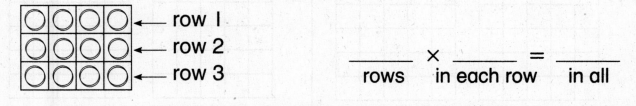

← row 1
← row 2
← row 3

_____ × _____ = _____
rows   in each row   in all

Color to count. Write a multiplication sentence for your count.

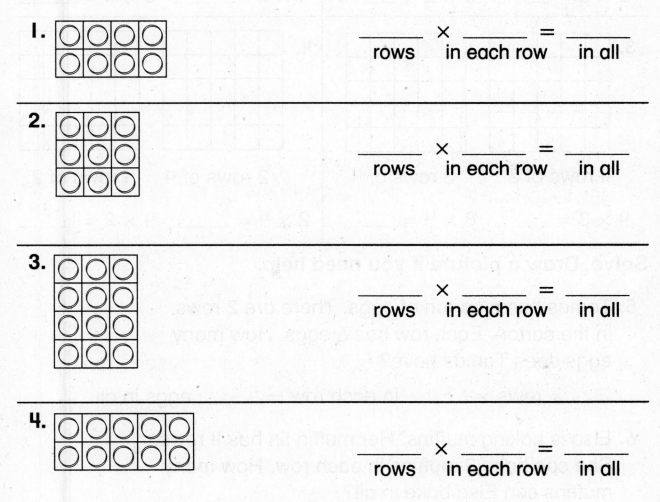

1.

_____ × _____ = _____
rows   in each row   in all

2.

_____ × _____ = _____
rows   in each row   in all

3.

_____ × _____ = _____
rows   in each row   in all

4.

_____ × _____ = _____
rows   in each row   in all

Name _____

Skills Practice

Arrays

Color the array. Find the product.

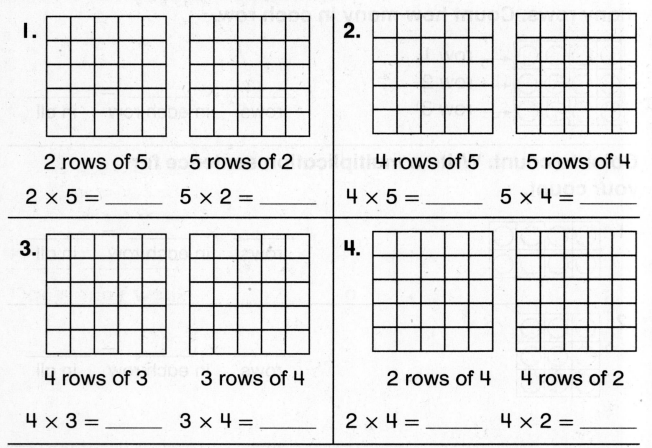

1.

2 rows of 5   5 rows of 2

$2 \times 5 =$ _____ $5 \times 2 =$ _____

2.

4 rows of 5   5 rows of 4

$4 \times 5 =$ _____ $5 \times 4 =$ _____

3.

4 rows of 3   3 rows of 4

$4 \times 3 =$ _____ $3 \times 4 =$ _____

4.

2 rows of 4   4 rows of 2

$2 \times 4 =$ _____ $4 \times 2 =$ _____

Solve. Draw a picture if you need help.

5. Tomás has a carton of eggs. There are 2 rows in the carton. Each row has 6 eggs. How many eggs does Tomás have?

_____ rows × _____ in each row = _____ eggs in all

6. Elsa is baking muffins. Her muffin tin has 4 rows. She can bake 3 muffins in each row. How many muffins can Elsa bake in all?

_____ rows × _____ in each row = _____ muffins in all

Name _____

Reteach

Division Stories

You can draw a picture to help.

There are 15 bananas.
There are 5 bananas in a bunch.
How many bunches are there?

Draw dots to show the first number.

Cross out groups of the second number.
Count how many Xs to solve.

There are ___3___ bunches.

Solve. Draw a picture to help.   **Show Your Work**

1. 20 people are on teams.
   There are 5 people on each team.

   How many teams can you have?

   _____ teams

---

2. 15 students share rides to school.
   There are 3 students in each car.

   How many cars do they take?

   _____ cars

---

3. Tim's grandpa is here for 28 days.
   There are 7 days in each week.

   How many weeks is Tim's grandpa
   here?

   _____ weeks

Name _____

Skills Practice

Division Stories

Model using ◯. Draw a picture to show your work.

1. 4 bowls hold

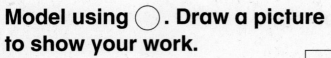

Each bowl holds

_____ cherries.

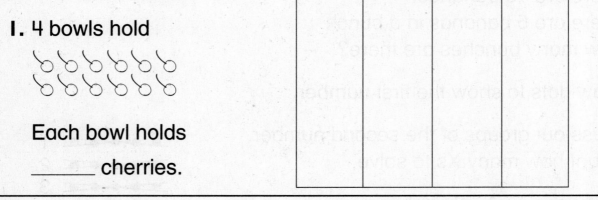

2. 3 bowls hold

Each bowl holds

_____ apples.

Use cubes to solve.

3. Sally has 16 blocks. She puts them into groups of 2.
   How many equal groups of 2 does Sally have?

   _____ ÷ _____ = _____

4. Tanya has 20 beads. She puts them into groups of 4.
   How many equal groups of 4 does Tanya have?

   _____ ÷ _____ = _____

Name _____

Reteach

Find Equal Groups

Color to make equal groups.

Make each group a new color.

6 ○

3 equal groups

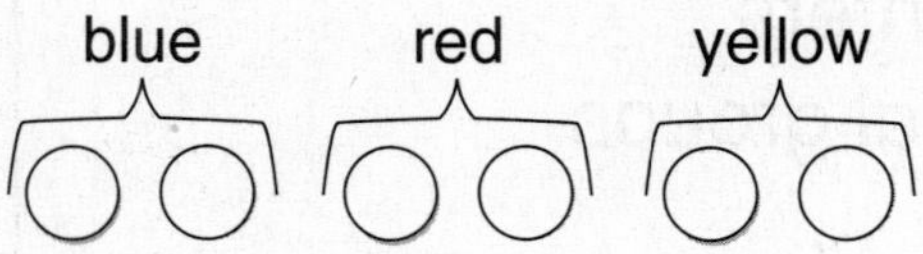

__2__ in each group

blue   red   yellow

__6__ ÷ __3__ = _____

Color to make equal groups. Write how many in each group. Divide.

1. 10 ○

5 equal groups

_____ in each group

_____ ÷ _____ = _____

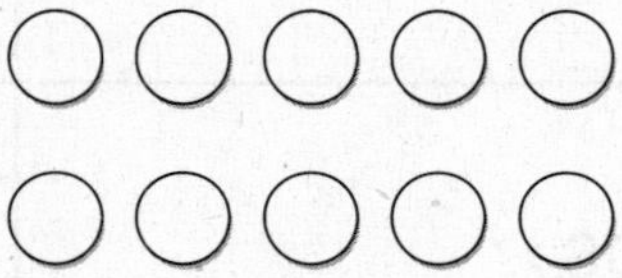

2. 14 ○

2 equal groups

_____ in each group

_____ ÷ _____ = _____

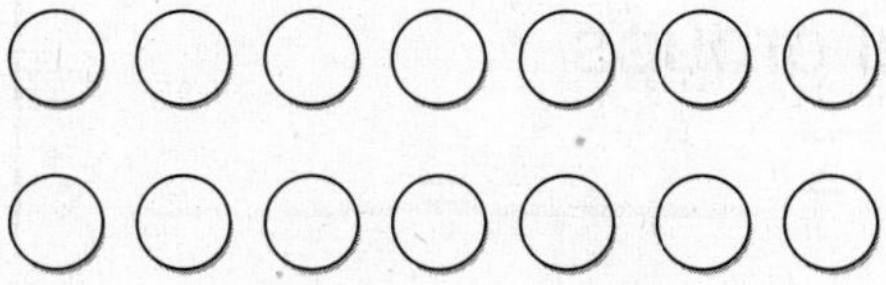

3. 8 ○

4 equal groups

_____ in each group

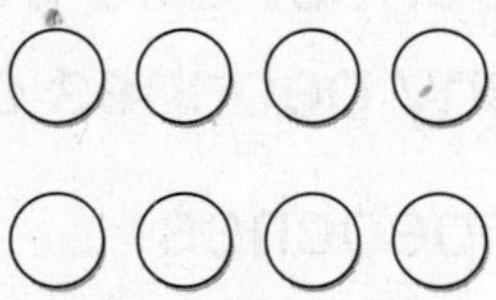

_____ ÷ _____ = _____

Name _____

Skills Practice

Find Equal Groups

**Model using counters to make equal groups.
How many are in each group? Divide.**

1. 6 counters
2 equal groups

_____ ÷ _____ = _____

2. 18 counters
9 equal groups

_____ ÷ _____ = _____

3. 20 counters
4 equal groups

_____ ÷ _____ = _____

4. 12 counters
4 equal groups

_____ ÷ _____ = _____

5. 15 counters
5 equal groups

_____ ÷ _____ = _____

6. 16 counters
2 equal groups

_____ ÷ _____ = _____

7. 18 counters
6 equal groups

_____ ÷ _____ = _____

8. 25 counters
5 equal groups

_____ ÷ _____ = _____

Solve.

9. Leslie has 24 peaches. She put equal groups of peaches into 3 bowls. How many peaches are in each bowl?

24 ÷ 3 = _____ peaches

10. Mr. Chan wrote 20 pages. He divided the pages into 4 equal chapters. How many pages are in each chapter?

20 ÷ 4 = _____ pages

Name _____

Reteach (1)

Problem-Solving Investigation: Choose a Strategy

Gabe has 3 shelves.
Each shelf has 7 books.
How many total books does Gabe have?

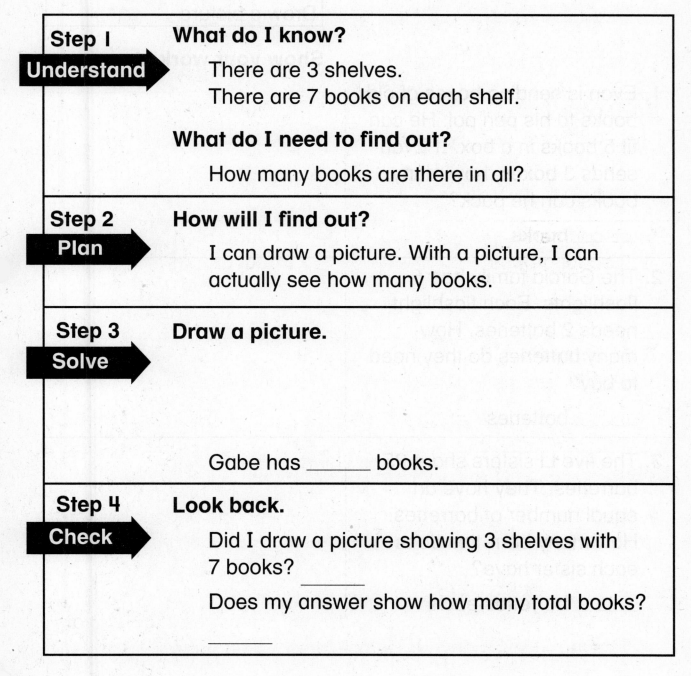

Step 1
Understand

What do I know?

There are 3 shelves.
There are 7 books on each shelf.

What do I need to find out?

How many books are there in all?

Step 2
Plan

How will I find out?

I can draw a picture. With a picture, I can actually see how many books.

Step 3
Solve

Draw a picture.

Gabe has _____ books.

Step 4
Check

Look back.

Did I draw a picture showing 3 shelves with 7 books? _____

Does my answer show how many total books? _____

Name _____

Reteach (2)

Problem-Solving Investigation: Choose a Strategy

Choose a strategy. Solve.

Problem-Solving Strategies
Act it out
Find a pattern
Draw a picture

Show your work here.

1. Evan is sending boxes of old books to his pen pal. He can fit 5 books in a box. If Evan sends 3 boxes, how many books can he pack?

   _____ books

2. The Garcia family has 6 flashlights. Each flashlight needs 2 batteries. How many batteries do they need to buy?

   _____ batteries

3. The five Li sisters share 25 barrettes. They have an equal number of barrettes. How many barrettes does each sister have?

   _____ barrettes each

Name _____

Skills Practice

Problem-Solving Investigation: Choose a Strategy

Choose a strategy. Solve.

> **Problem-Solving Strategies**
> Act it out
> Find a pattern
> Draw a picture

1. Seven cousins share 14 friendship bracelets. They each have the same number of bracelets.

How many bracelets does each cousin have?

_____ bracelets

2. Abby made 12 dollars babysitting.
She babysat for 3 hours.

How many dollars did Abby make each hour?

_____ dollars

3. Devon feeds his three rabbits 15 carrots. Each rabbit eats the same number of carrots.

How many carrots does each rabbit eat?

_____ carrots

What if Devon fed the rabbits 18 carrots?

_____ carrots

4. Liam made 6 pies.
Each pie has 3 apples.

How many apples did Liam use in all?

_____ apples

How many apples would Liam need for 8 pies?

_____ apples